A BARRISTER'S TALES

REVIEWS

~

"*A Barrister's Tales* contains riveting tales told by a master yarn spinner. I couldn't put it down."

Orson Bean, Actor, Director, Producer & Author

"*A Barrister's Tales* is entertaining, witty, unpredictable and profound. Nichols' storytelling pulls you into his worlds and never lets you go until each memoir makes its mark on you. From the 1929 Depression-era to the rise of Hollywood in the thirties, to the radical 60s and into the world of law and justice—it tells the tales of a sardonic lawyer on a spiritual journey toward God's providence."

Brian Godawa, Bestselling author, *Chronicles of the Nephilim*

"*A Barrister's Tales* is a book that is likely to touch all hearts —but particularly the skeptical—in a powerful way. I was mesmerized by how God worked in Cliff's life to get his attention. Too many people believe God doesn't exist or if He does He's not involved in their every day lives. The truth is God created each of us for a special purpose and to be in a relationship with Him. If you doubt this is true, I dare you to read this book! Hopefully you will see a little bit of yourself and your life's experiences in these stories. And for the rest who already have a relationship with Papa God, this book will build your faith. Truly, a good read."

Amanda Pecott, Psalm139LOVE Ministries, Haiti

A BARRISTER'S TALES

ONE LAWYER'S MEMOIRS OF HIS JOURNEY
TOWARD FAITH ALONG A TRAIL
CALLED LIFE

CLIFFORD C. NICHOLS

CHEZ MOI PRESS™

Scripture taken from the NEW AMERICAN
STANDARD BIBLE(R), Copyright (C)
1960,1962,1963,1968,1971,1972,1973,1975,1977,1995
by The Lockman Foundation. Used by permission.

Edited by Jeanette Windle, jeanettewindle.com
Cover Design by Lynda Nichols, cooldogdesign.com
Cover Photo by Dino Reichmuth on Unsplash

ISBN 13: 978-0-578-57011-2
Chez Moi Press™
Published in the United States of America
First Edition 2019

The noble man devises noble plans.[1]

DEDICATION

To those looking back on their journey who—like me—see certain events were signposts directing them toward an ordained end not fully appreciated until they had arrived.

To all others—including my children—who differ only in that much of their journey remains before them.

To Papa

The mind of man plans his way, but the Lord directs his steps.[2]

CONTENTS

~

OPENING ARGUMENT

He has told you, O man, what is good;
and what does the Lord require of you,
but to do justice, to love kindness, and
to walk humbly with your God?[1]

~

Many are the plans in a man's heart, but the counsel of the Lord will stand. [1]

A NOTE FROM THE AUTHOR

I would do well to advise you that several of the chapters in this book include adult language and descriptions that conceivably could adversely impact some readers. For their convenience these chapters have been identified by the symbol ≠ following the chapter title. That said, however, please also note that in my opinion the relevant passages in these chapters have been toned down to the degree necessary to placate most readers while, at the same time, also permit the Tales to remain grounded in truth.

Readers are further advised that artistic license has been employed here and there throughout the telling of these Tales. When and where appropriate or necessary, names, times and places have been changed and characters and events have been combined to serve at least one and sometimes two purposes: (i) to ease the flow in telling some of the Tales; and (ii) to protect the innocence or disguise the possible guilt of some who were involved.

By and large, however, the reader can be assured that all of the Tales I am about to tell are firmly grounded in true events that actually did impact the lives of very real people.

    With that said, let the Tales be loosed.

You will know the truth, and the truth will make you free.[2]

THE TRUTH AND NOTHING BUT THE TRUTH

~

You have searched us and known us. You know when we sit down and when we rise up; You understand our thoughts from afar. You scrutinize our paths and our lying down, and are intimately acquainted with all our ways. Even before there are words on our tongues ... You knew it all. [1]

Look not at the things which are seen, but at the things which are not seen; for the things which are seen are temporal, but the things which are not seen are eternal. [2]

If you continue in his word, then ... you will know the truth, and the truth will make you free. [3]

~

The kingdom of heaven is like a mustard seed, which ... is smaller than all other seeds, but when it is full grown, it ... becomes a tree.[1]

∿

1

A SEED PLANTED

"Son, no matter where your life takes you, always remember that if you have eyes willing to see and ears willing to hear, you will come to find *you are never traveling alone.*"

With that non sequitur, my paternal granddad—who we all called Papa—went to bed with a smile on his face.

Was this his idea of a joke? He tells me I'll never be alone as he leaves me sitting there on his porch—alone—to finish the whiskey in my hand he just poured.

Not likely. Papa was not the joking kind.

But he was the kind of guy who liked dropping pearls of wisdom into the comparatively empty noggins of young kids like me. Thinking back now, it's pretty safe to say he was probably counting on this particular pearl rattling around in there like a loose pebble, hoping it would plague my fifteen-year-old brain long after he was gone. Which, I must confess, it did.

Papa was good at doing things like that. As he left the

porch that night, all I remember thinking was, *What the heck is that supposed to mean?*

Even then I was pretty sure it had something to do with the God Papa was always talking about. But I had no way of knowing that for me to arrive at a meaningful answer to my question would take thirty years of living and bring me to putting my arm around the shoulders of a young woman in court one day who at that moment seemed more like she wanted to die than live.

The ... seed ... sown among the thorns, ... is the man who hears the word, and the worry of the world and the deceitfulness of wealth choke the word, and it becomes unfruitful. [2]

Then God said, "Let us make man in our image ... and let them rule over ... the cattle.[1]

~

2

THE GENESIS OF IT ALL

From the title of this book, you may have guessed by now that I am an attorney, not a doctor, actor, full-time cowboy, or mortician. With my family's background, I can assure you most of the latter were no accident!

My growing up years—when I wasn't with Papa for the summer—were spent in a big home on a fashionable street in Los Angeles with a doctor for a dad, a housewife for a mom, two brothers, two sisters, and an unending series of dogs.

We lived large, close to the Pacific Ocean and a number of successful actors.

From time to time we would encounter some of these actors walking their various breeds of canines along with their most recent spouses through the tree-lined streets of the neighborhood. Growing up, I found myself wondering which they replaced more often—their spouses or their dogs.

Perhaps that's one reason why my dad was so set against his children even considering the entertainment field for a career. Though he had other reasons as well.

"Good people don't go into acting," he repeated periodically throughout our childhood. "Actors spend a lot more time on the casting couch than most will ever spend in front of a camera."

I wouldn't fully appreciate all the implications of this until I was well into my teens. But his general drift was always clear to me even as a pre-pubescent child. He didn't think much of actors, and so far as career choices, acting was pretty near the bottom of his totem pole.

I figured Dad knew what he was talking about. He'd grown up during the Great Depression, and when the economic forces of those times crossed paths with the circumstances of his childhood, he was compelled for one brief period to become an actor—or almost one.

As the story went, Papa brought his wife and four sons to Los Angeles from a little town near El Paso, Texas in 1929 in search of work. I came to learn later that this explanation of their journey west was only that part of the truth my grandparents chose to offer to the public—that is, those nosey church people who couldn't refrain from asking about things that weren't any of their business. The whole truth turns out to be a bit more like the following.

My grandparents were born sometime in the late 1890s into a small Texan community where my grandmother's family had hovered for decades not far above bankruptcy by ranching cattle on land the good Lord never blessed with much grass. The business plan ranchers in that part of the country seemed to operate on was that if the cattle had to almost starve much of the year, it was only right the cowboys who insisted on putting them there should also have to go hungry. And go hungry they often did.

Add to this that my grandmother was apparently born without the requisite genetic makeup necessary to form any emotional attachment to a lifestyle that revolved around things like boots, spurs, and ropes, much less the cowboy hats she often said reminded her of empty taco shells.

It didn't help that neither my grandmother or Papa were particularly pleased with his job at the time. He and his brother worked for his dad—my great-grandfather—who was the town mortician.

Their job included picking up the bodies of anyone in the county who happened to die, bringing them into town for burial, then digging the holes for that to happen. Needless to say, they also had to close the holes back up afterwards. It made for long days for little pay. But if that were not enough, one additional factor gave both brothers an incentive to look for alternative career paths.

Quite literally, the job stunk!

Papa started working for his dad shortly after Teddy Roosevelt's presidency (1901-1909), and cars were still new enough to the American way of life that Teddy was the first president to ever ride in one.

So how did this fact impact Papa's world?

Mainly because even after Teddy left the White House,

cars were still scarce enough—especially in the poorer parts of rural towns in states like Texas—that the transportation end of my great granddad's funeral service operation consisted entirely of a buckboard wagon and a couple of tired old horses. Since many of his customers died on farms or ranches inconveniently far from town, Papa and his brother were left hauling the cadavers back to town in the company buckboard. Such trips could take an entire day.

As Papa told it many years later, the trips weren't so bad in winter, but summer was a different story. Temperatures often reached in excess of 115 degrees, and a dead body jostling around in a wagon bed in the baking sun did nothing to improve the smell of somebody already dead for a day or two.

Papa never did develop the ability to keep from throwing up from time to time. But he sure did develop a new regard for the life of a buzzard. In fact, he once suggested to me someone's similar experience must have spawned the expression that something was so disgusting "it would cause a buzzard sitting on a %#&! wagon to pass out."

Suffice it to say, the life of a rural mortician wasn't a skill set either of my paternal grandparents saw as providing a bright future for them or their four sons, of whom my dad was the third born. My grandmother also knew that if her husband sought another career path in that particular area of near El Paso, it would likely involve ranching. And with her family background, she was well aware this would only guarantee being just as poor as the son of a mortician.

So about the time my dad's youngest brother reached school age—and shortly after my grandparents had managed to buy their first car—my grandmother informed her friends, loved-ones, *and* her husband, Papa, that whether they or he liked it or not, her family was going to pack up and leave for Los Angeles.

When her family or any other local asked her why, she declared decades before Willie Nelson ever thought to sing about it, "I don't want my boys growing up to be cowboys."

This made complete sense to her, and that some of the cowboys she was telling this to might be offended evidently didn't matter. She was soon packed up and headed to Los Angeles with her husband and four boys in tow. Behind them as they took off down the dirt road, loved ones and friends could be seen in the car's rear-view mirror chewing lengths of straw and shaking their heads.

These people took what comfort they could by telling each other in their Texan country drawls, "They'll be back, mark my words! . . . Yup, y'all just wait and see . . . Likely with their tails tucked between their legs, yessiree!"

But the friends and loved-ones were wrong—at least for a good long while. Upon their arrival in the Golden State, chance, opportunity, or in their view Providence led my grandparents to rent a house just off a street named Gower in a place called Hollywood. This just happened to be in the same neighborhood as some buildings even folks back home had heard about that people called *moving picture studios*. Specifically, the Gower Studios.

At the time my grandparents arrived in Hollywood, making movies was a fledgling industry people like them knew little about and cared about even less. By then Papa was in his early thirties—a strapping 6'4" former dead body hauler, hole digger and filler-back-upper, and wannabe cowboy. The thought of letting a makeup artist put powder on his nose, much less acting like someone he wasn't in front of a camera, wasn't remotely a part of the universe in which he and my grandmother lived. In tough times like this, real men like my grandfather had to man up, get going, and make a real living.

Papa was thrilled to land a fairly low-paying job selling meat for a meat processing company not far from their new residence. Years later, he told me he got the job in large part because the owner of the processing plant liked two facts. First, Papa had apparently given the impression he knew something about cows, leaving out that he'd typically seen them only at a distance while hauling dead people cross-country. Secondly, the owner was impressed that Papa had just driven all the way from Texas.

To the owner, these two facts meant Papa knew the product the company sold and the very road on which the company would hire him to sell it. In short order, Papa was commissioned to travel back and forth from Los Angeles to El Paso, selling all the meat he could to any restaurant, hotel, or grocer he crossed paths with in between.

Not that he sold literal meat. He would take the orders,

call them in to his boss, and the company would then ship the beef.

I'm not sure whether the irony of his new career ever occurred to Papa. His wife had moved from a town by El Paso to get him away from cattle. Instead, he'd ended up selling cattle—or at least the beef those cattle produced— all the way back to El Paso.

If the irony did occur to him, he never mentioned it in my presence, and it never occurred to me to ask until long after he was gone. Not that I'd have had the courage to ask while he was still in the land of the living. Papa was not known for having an appreciation for such ironies—or for that matter, as I've already mentioned, much of a sense of humor of any sort.

Eventually, Papa did reveal something else about those early years I found as unsettling as his non sequitur about *never traveling in life alone*. It would appear meat wasn't all he sold as he traveled along on his appointed trail to Texas and back. This was still the Prohibition era (abolished in 1933), and it seemed many of his customers liked booze as much as they did meat. Papa was soon making extra money dropping off bottles of booze to "special" customers from cases he kept hidden in his back trunk.

He told me about this side business one evening during my early teens as we sipped on glasses of the bourbon whiskey he so enjoyed of an evening. I found it interesting that he acknowledged no moral difference between commissions he earned selling legal beef and money derived from the selling of illegal booze.

I must confess this bothered me because I'd always known both of my grandparents to be firmly devoted to the Good Book. Plus I'd been raised to believe good Christians didn't commit crimes. So this random factoid my grandfather laid on me just didn't fit into the image I had of him. Ironically, that I myself was technically breaking the law as I sat there sipping whiskey while well under the legal drinking age never crossed my mind.

"Weren't you a Christian back then?" I asked.

"Sure was," he responded nonchalantly as though why would I doubt it.

"But you were a bootlegger! If you were a Christian, how could you possibly justify doing illegal stuff like that? It's not even possible to be a good Christian bootlegger, is it?"

His answer was simple, unapologetic, and given without hesitation. "You wouldn't know what it was like, but Prohibition era was also the Great Depression, and times back then were tough. When a man is on the road trying to make a living and he's got a wife and four boys he loves back home who need to eat, then so long as nobody gets hurt or killed, he can't be blamed for doing whatever he needs to do to keep them fed."

Well, I couldn't argue with that, and so that was the end of that discussion. But it does bring me back to our subject at hand—why acting was never a viable career choice for me. Or more particularly, how I came to become an attorney.

During those Depression years, my grandmother was as busy as Papa doing what she could—at least within those confines of decency dictated by her sincere belief that God was watching everything she did—to make sure the rent was paid and her children didn't go hungry in between the arrival of her husband's commission checks. Initially this involved sewing, cleaning, and cooking to bring in a few extra pennies.

But my grandmother eventually got wind that extra money could always be made around this town named Hollywood through what to her was just one more form of odd job—hiring her sons out as extras to some of the nearby *moving picture studios* when opportunities came up for bit parts. This involved doing what they did naturally— playing around as kids—but getting paid for it. In short order, my dad and his brothers found themselves playing minor non-speaking roles such as kids in the background for productions like the *Our Gang* series, which was filmed at the Roach Studios located in nearby Culver City.

Let me make clear that this wasn't because my grand-mother had been swept away by the rising glamour of Hollywood movie making. She most definitely was not one of those infamous "stage moms" who hung around the studios hoping their child would be "discovered." But in her book, even acting was a better thing for her boys to be doing—at least while they were young—than growing up to be cowboys.

According to Papa, there was never a time in all of this that he or my grandmother ever wanted their sons to become "stars." So it was no big deal to them when a cocky little kid from down the street named Mickey Rooney, who also worked as an occasional extra, became a rising young star and moved out of the neighborhood. As far as Papa was concerned, this just meant the kid wouldn't be sneaking into their living room anymore on Saturday mornings to bang on the family piano or coaxing my father and his three brothers outside to play some noisy game when all Papa wanted was to sleep in after a long week on the road selling meat.

As my father and his brothers headed outside to play with young Mickey, none of them could have guessed that the trajectory of their futures would take them worlds away from the kind of life Mickey Rooney would experience in the years that followed. Nor did they have any idea that for all practical purposes their fate had already been sealed in the mind of my grandmother. They weren't going to be movie stars but something far better—at least to my grand-mother's way of thinking. They were going to become *doctors*.

Why? Because that's what she had decided was the very best thing they, or anyone else for that matter, could possibly do this side of heaven short of attaining deification.

This could also very well explain why my father came to believe that "good people don't go into acting." My grandmother undoubtedly indoctrinated her four sons in this mantra on a regular basis growing up—most likely on Sundays going to or from church.

The flip side of that coin was that they were also *gently* led by her to believe with every fiber of their being that those who are indeed righteous must become doctors. In the end, they all did. Though for my dad at least, it wasn't always such a clear path.

Specifically, it seems that at one point he had developed the aberrant desire of wanting to become an attorney. In fact, so insistent was he on this break from his predestined trajectory that for a while in his college years he took pre-law courses. I'm told he excelled at these and won some national award for his ability to debate. But that was all before World War II hit him like a ton of bricks.

For his military service, Dad was assigned as a federal government surveyor in the forests of Oregon. By the time he returned to civilian life almost four years later, several key factors had played a role in his ultimate decision as to what to do with the rest of his life.

He had apparently emerged from the forests at some point during the war long enough to meet my mother and get married. While he was away, all three of his brothers had become doctors with the help of deferments coupled with scholarships. And all three joined my grandmother (and presumably my grandfather) in a unified chorus to encourage my dad to do likewise now that he was back.

It turned out, however, that it wasn't all that easy.

Due to competition from countless soldiers being discharged from the military, it turned out that *wanting* to get into medical school and actually *getting* in were two very different things. No matter how hard my dad tried and notwithstanding my grandparents' continual prayers, one discouragement after another stacked up until one day my dad found himself sitting on a rock in the front yard of his folk's home in total despair. Another medical school had rejected him, and he was almost in tears.

Just then, an elderly man in a wheelchair rolled himself down the street, saw my dad, and stopped to talk with him. My dad had seen this man around the neighborhood in his wheelchair, but never gave him much thought.

The old man lifted his gray-haired head above his stooped shoulders. He waited until my dad made eye contact, then asked why he looked so sad. My dad explained his most recent medical school rejection. The old man listened until he finished, then said, "You know, if you don't mind, I'd like to see your undergraduate grades. And your résumé if you have one."

"Why?" my dad asked in surprise. What could this old man possibly want with his grades—or do if he got them?

"Well, you never know," the old man responded. "Maybe there's something I could do to help. If I can, I will. It can't hurt to try."

My dad did as the old man requested. Several months later, he received a letter from the dean of the University of Chicago School of Medicine. It informed him he'd been admitted for the coming school year and needed to get there right away. Classes started in just three days.

The old man in the wheelchair turned out to have been one of the dean's teachers back in high school and for reasons we'll never really know agreed that my dad would be a good doctor.

A miracle?

My dad and Papa always believed it to be one, and so they told us kids. But, at the time Papa first told me this story, I must confess I thought miracles were just the Christian version of *good luck*, and so for the longest time I assumed that's what he meant.

At the end of the day, as I've already mentioned, my dad did become a physician. But in another of those small ironies of life, I find it fascinating that the first thing he did once he was on sound financial footing (after completing medical school, not to mention all the residencies and internships that followed) was to buy himself a "ranch" outside of Los Angeles. This he kept stocked at all times with a variety of horses and never more or less than one cow.

That's right, one cow.

When one cow ended up on the barbecue, he'd always replace it with another. And the "cowboy" my dad put in charge of his ranch operation? None other than my grandfather, Papa, whom my grandmother had always forbidden to even think of becoming a cowboy.

It bears mentioning that my grandmother had already passed away at the age of sixty-three shortly before my dad acquired the ranch. From her teens, she'd suffered from a form of arthritis that made her days painful—some more than others. I have often wondered if this was not a reason she wanted her boys to become doctors. Though notwithstanding all their medical degrees, it became evident they remained helpless to relieve her of her arthritis and the extreme pain it brought, especially toward the end of her life.

One night when she was lying in bed next to my grandfather, her pain became so intense that Papa heard her audibly asking God to take her home to heaven. God listened to her pleas that very night. So it was that Papa was left to his own devices to be a cowboy for the remaining ten years of his own life until God allowed him to rejoin my grandmother.

To this day, my memory of Papa during the summers I spent with him on the ranch were the evenings. He always had a scripture or two to quote in the course of telling me a few stories as he sipped his whiskey and smoked a cigarette or two with a smile on his face.

I doubt the irony of his life coming full circle was lost on even him. He was now the cowboy he had always wanted to be, even if the herd he was charged to care for consisted of only one cow. Was that too a miracle on par with my dad getting into medical school, or just Papa's turn to experience some good luck? Who knew? Papa most certainly never mentioned it as such, and at the time I was just happy he no longer had to do things like hide booze in the trunk of his car.

So, now you now know how I came to be raised in a family that—long before my birth and notwithstanding my dad's ranch and the cow that came with it—had ruled out the options of my ever becoming an actor, a mortician or a full-time cowboy.

You may also better appreciate how anyone raised in my family with no interest in pursuing medicine really had just one other viable career choice: *the practice of law.*

Practically speaking, it was the only profession other than medicine my dad would have been willing to help fund. And so it was upon my graduation from high school now over fifty years ago that I started down this seemingly predestined path called *life*.

And that is pretty much the starting gate from whence my journey began.

～

*Train up a child in the way he should go,
even when he is old he will not depart from it.*[2]

God ... make me walk on high places.[1]

~

3

AN UPHILL CLIMB

Along with his one cow, my dad kept a rotating stock of three to four quarter horses on his ranch at any given time. Primarily these horses came from one of two sources.

One source was other doctors who had horses they wanted to get rid of because they'd grown tired of feeding them as well as their fantasies of becoming either cowboys or racetrack champions.

The others were donated by my father's cousins near El Paso, who were still cowboys engaged in the fantasy of making a living on the family ranch. Since that time, these cousins had taken to breeding and selling a line of champion palominos. Fortunately for us, this new endeavor necessitated getting rid of any foal with a genetic blemish that could hurt the breeder's reputation—like the occasional albino foal.

To me, it didn't matter where they came from. I was the only one among my siblings who wanted much of anything to do with horses or for that matter my dad's ranch at all. From the time I was in junior high school, whatever else I was or would become, I was—in my own mind at least—a cowboy, albeit a cowboy with only one cow.

Of course at the beginning of my teenage career as a caballero, Papa was still in charge of his herd of one cow. But that cow rarely—read *never*—needed to be moved anywhere beyond the corral it called home until the family freezer became empty again. So for the most part, I was left to ride alone without having to worry about things like cattle stampedes or needless conversation.

For me, riding for miles in the desert through the outcroppings of the occasional rolling hills that surrounded the ranch soon evolved into a passion that transformed in the course of my youth into a kind of therapy. If nothing else, it put me out alone in places where I could think, shoot an occasional jackrabbit, and hope I didn't get bucked off before I got back to the ranch. During my teen years, it just couldn't get much better than that.

But with the passage of time, things changed as they tend to do. I graduated from high school at seventeen and was getting ready to go off to college in the fall. By then I had also discovered a species of greater interest to me than horses—co-eds in the miniskirts and go-go boots of that era. All of which left me more interested that summer in heading to the beach to eyeball girls than riding horses.

In consequence, that summer was also the first since my grandmother's death that Papa was left to tend the ranch all on his own. This was a sad and lonely season for him, though I wasn't really aware of it at the time. That fall, I headed off to college and somewhere along the way turned eighteen.

I was just getting used to living in my college dormitory when my dad called late one evening to let me know that Papa had followed Grandma on down the trail she'd blazed ahead of him ten years earlier. Interestingly, even that was not to be without some portion of irony. I learned from Dad his remains would be laid next to those of my grandmother in the cemetery of the very same small town they had both fled some forty years before to come to Los Angeles. But that didn't hit me until later. So, in the end, after all was said and done, they did come back after all.

That evening, after Dad hung up, I cried as the news of Papa's death sunk in. It was as though he'd walked into the sunset he so loved to watch, but this time he wouldn't be coming back. Later I often wondered if anyone thought to check for the whiskey I'm sure he had hidden in his trunk as he passed through the Pearly Gates.

My dad hired another caretaker and kept the ranch in operation for many years afterward. Which allowed me the opportunity even after Papa's death to continue riding from time to time and sort through the memories of the stories he had told that I would take with me for the rest of my life.

One such story was about the lean years before my grandparents left the El Paso territory when times were tough and money for food was scarce. He and a few of his buddies began thinking about all the deer residing outside of town in the mountains beyond the ranches. More than enough to provide the meat their families were craving. Why let it go to waste?

So Papa and his pals would load up a buckboard and traipse up to the mountains for about a week at a time, camping out and hunting all the deer they needed for their families. This they repeated whenever a consensus formed that hunger had again raised its ugly head.

There was only one problem. Their families' need to eat didn't always coincide exactly with the state's designated deer hunting season. But that didn't bother anyone too much. Their need to eat trumped their need for a hunting permit, so the risk was worth it. An added benefit for him and his buddies in doing it as *outlaws* was turning what otherwise would have been an ordinary hunting trip into an *adventure* embarked upon by a posse of desperados.

All they had to worry about was making sure it was cold enough to keep the meat from going bad on the way home—and not getting caught. When Papa told me this story decades later, he admitted with a chuckle that hiding the meat in burlap sacks buried under their camping gear in the back of the buckboard was probably not the best plan for avoiding detection should they ever have actually crossed paths with any authorities—i.e. game wardens— along their way home.

While hardly an example of the perfect crime, it was at least evidence of the scientific fact that the cerebral cortex of the average male does not fully form until they get to be somewhere around twenty-five years old!

Which puts me in mind of a twenty-one-year-old young man I represented years later. In the course of his brief criminal career while employed as an assistant in a Brink's armored cash transport truck, he also formed a less than perfect plan in his not yet fully formed mind to steal some money from his employer. One day at some point along their regular route where he could be confident the driver wouldn't see him, he would toss a bag of cash out the back of the armored truck to where a buddy would be waiting in a car.

His plan went well at first. The cash handoff was accomplished successfully, and the driver of the armored truck didn't see or hear a thing. It couldn't get any better!

That was until the tally came up one bag short at the daily bag count taken that evening back at headquarters. When the police were called in, they of course undertook to search the cars and houses of those Brink employees who had worked that day. Needless to say, this included my client's home.

Interestingly, it wasn't that my client hadn't anticipated this possibility and even planned for it. His problem was that his less than well-formed cerebral cortex never imagined the police would think to look under the dirty clothes in his bathroom hamper—whereas per his carefully thought-out plan he had hidden the bag of cash. Go figure!

Before returning to this chapter's main narrative, I would be remiss not to mention that the truly astonishing finale of this anecdote was not how impressed the young man proved to be with the amazing "cleverness" of the police but the judge's phenomenal leniency when sentencing my client. I could only conclude the judge felt some level of sympathy for just how stupid this kid and his plan had been. Yes, it was a crime. But all involved in the case were left feeling that for this client and his buddy it had been an adventure only a couple of kids could dream up while waiting for their cerebral cortices to finally catch up to the rest of their development.

The point of all this is to make clear I myself was not immune to such flawed thought patterns in my youth. But like my client and most others of that age group, I also was not aware of my mental deficiencies at the time. In fact, I have to wonder if Papa was aware in telling me of adventures like his outlaw hunting trips the effect such stories were having on my young brain. He might as well have been pouring gasoline on the burning twigs of a yet not fully formed yet smoldering mind.

Which brings me to a time shortly after Papa passed away when I decided in his memory to push the envelope and seek the thrill of an adventure that at least in my mind was somewhat akin to his illicit deer hunting trips. This involved taking a horseback journey of my own to the snow-dusted crest of the mountains twenty-seven miles from my folks' ranch.

I realize that twenty-seven miles might not seem any great distance, and it isn't by car. But on horseback, it's forever. Round trip, that's fifty-four miles. It took me weeks to plan and prepare for—food, camping gear, and water supplies, not only for me but the horses, etc. All had to be considered. Anything overlooked could present a serious problem.

Eventually, my preparations were complete. So early

one Saturday morning, good idea or not, I took off. I had with me to accomplish this feat my two favorite geldings.

I rode one with my Marlin .38 caliber lever action rifle in a saddle scabbard secured to my cinch. Of all the weapons my family owned for hunting, the .38 was the one I thought best for the trip I was making. The ammunition was cheap and not too big. But not too small either, making it a perfect varmint gun for jackrabbits, snakes, or coyotes. More importantly, it was a lever action rifle similar in appearance to the vintage 30-30's used by true cowboys. Or at least by those who portrayed those cowboys in Hollywood westerns. So far as I was concerned, if a rifle that looked like my .38 was good enough for Clint Eastwood to use for shooting bad guys, that mere fact made it something well worth hauling around Hell's Half-Acre on my own adventure.

My second horse carried the food, sleeping bag, and cooking gear necessary for me to brave the wilderness I intended to explore.

At first the trek led across miles of flat desert floor that stretched from our ranch to the base of the mountain I intended to climb. I'd planned to be climbing the mountain by a little after noon that day, but it took more hours than I thought just to reach the foothills. From that point, the trail I'd chosen took an increasingly uphill slant that eventually became quite steep.

The geldings and I plodded around and between boulders, oaks, sycamores, and an increasing number of pines to get to the trail I'd decided would get us to the top. Eventually the pines took over our surroundings, and the trail we ended up on left the oaks, sycamores, and desert shrubs to fade away in the rear-view mirror of my mind.

That's when I experienced a prescient feeling that the real adventure I'd embarked upon was about to start in earnest.

The forest trail leading toward the mountain crest was lonely, quiet, and at some points quite unnerving. Mostly uphill, it eventually became quite precipitous. The canyon gorges through which we traveled grew ever deeper and more narrow. The sun had already passed beyond their rims high above me, and the canyon depths were darkened further by the shade of the evergreen canopy under which my horses and I rode.

The methodical clinking of my horses' metal shoes striking rock as they trudged uphill coupled with the rhythmic whoosh of breath from their nostrils became hypnotic, causing my mind to drift toward other places and different people. Mainly I was considering proudly what some of my classmates—in particular the girls—would think if they could see me now.

In fact, I was so entranced in thought that I lost my focus on the trail until the horses came to an abrupt halt of their own accord, which brought my mind back to the present. I immediately grasped why they'd stopped. We had arrived at a section of the trail that led across a steep rock face. I had planned for this, but not for what had brought the horses to a standstill. What I found myself looking at sent my heart leaping into my throat.

Rushing water from some rainstorm had washed out a portion of the trail ahead and presented me with some interesting issues to be resolved—like what in tarnation we were going to do now! By stopping on their own, my horses clearly seemed to have decided this was a good point to look to me for some guidance. Perhaps they were thinking this trip had been my bright idea, so deciding what to do next should be more my problem than theirs.

On my right side, a rock wall so close that the granite scraped against my stirrup rose straight up to the canyon rim far above us. But it was the other side that offered the greater cause for concern. If nothing were pressing on my left stirrup, that was because it hovered over nothing but air that dropped almost straight down for what seemed like nearly a hundred feet. Between these two extremes, the trail wasn't wide enough to turn the horses around and head on back down the gorge toward home.

In the end, I was left with only one real choice. If all three of us were to make it out of here, we were all going to have to jump the gap.

Beneath me I could feel my horse's massive muscles shaking. Whether due to exhaustion because he'd had to work so hard to get this far up the trail or because the horse to some degree understood the danger we were in, I'll never know. All I knew for sure was that I'd first have to dismount. If either horse lost his footing and disappeared over the edge, the last place I wanted to be was somewhere that might force me to join it in a fall inevitably fatal for all concerned.

I had to dismount on the side overlooking the gorge while keeping a grip on both sets of reins. Slowly sliding down, I found my boots coming to rest on the trail with my heels hanging over the edge. I could feel a cool mountain breeze passing by on its way down the gorge, drying the sweat that was forming on my forehead.

As I let go of my lead horse's reins, I carefully slid along his body back to my packhorse. There I wrapped my second horse's lead rope around his halter's chin strap to prevent him from stepping on it while giving him at least some latitude of autonomy in what we were about to attempt. I then worked my way gingerly back to the front of the lead horse, where I took up that horse's reins. Without any delay that might allow me any time to chicken out, I jumped.

Making it to the other side, I then skipped and scrambled as quickly as I could up the trail to get out of the way of my horse should he choose to jump the gap with me, all the while without looking back. Quite simply, if either horse lost its footing, I didn't want to watch them disappear over the edge. My only hope for the horses—not to mention me and the continued success of my adventure— was that pulling on the lead gelding's reins would encourage both horses to attempt the gap I had just jumped on foot. Somebody had told me once that the intelligence of the smartest horse ever born was less than that of the dumbest dog. If that was true, it was anyone's guess whether my geldings would think jumping the gap was a good idea.

I should note that in the course of all this I never once thought of sending up a prayer. That might not have been a bad idea, but any thought of God would have to come later. I was too busy trying to save my life along with the lives of my horses.

As I scrambled far enough from the gap for my lead horse to have room to land, I felt the tension of the reins I was gripping go slack, telling me that my lead horse had indeed jumped the gap behind me. Then in what seemed like only a split second later, the second horse, not wanting to be left behind, followed suit and made the jump also.

A miracle? Perhaps.

Miraculous? Absolutely!

"Thank you, God!" I screamed to nobody in particular. Though it was basically a reflex, I'm glad I did that at least. But it was only a passing thought.

Long story short, we all crossed the gap without a hitch. Since we had no choice at this point, we continued on toward the canyon rim above us. I was hoping desperately there would be no more such gaps on the trail. But I was already forgetting God's possible contribution to our escape, my adrenaline-driven thoughts of gratitude soon being replaced with more self-indulgent thoughts like the following:

"Well, you wanted adventure, and that's what you've got. But this is STUPID! What were you thinking? If nothing else, I sure hope there's a different trail I can take to get back home. There's gotta be, right? I'm sure there will be. No need to worry about it now. I'll figure it out when the time comes. At least, I hope so!"

Eventually, the adrenaline and the thoughts it was generating subsided as the horses and I continued on in solitary tranquility. About an hour later—that being seven or eight hours since we'd begun this adventure—the three of us finally topped out onto a mountain ridge from which I could see my family's ranch far out in the distance below.

The horses were tired, and so was I. But the incredible panoramic view spreading out below the ridge made our adventure well worth the ride. At least it did for me. I'm pretty sure the horses were somewhat less enthralled.

The campground where I'd planned to spend the night was now just a couple of miles east along the ridge. From here the trail would be relatively level so the hard part of our trek was done.

Since the sun was still two or three hours from setting, I decided that the horses—not to mention my rear end— had earned a short rest before beginning the last leg to the campground.

At least that was the plan.

Dismounting, I led the horses into a dirt parking lot off to one side of a nearby dirt road that allowed vehicles to access the ridge we were on. The lot provided easy access for day hikers to any number of trails converging there from either direction along the ridge and down into various canyons. From the trail map tacked to a Forest Service bulletin board, I could now see that I had various options to choose from when it was time for the horses and me to head home.

Needless to say, this was a discovery that made me happy. In fact, it thrilled me. Hopefully, this time I could find a trail that wouldn't necessitate jumping a gap or any other such drama. Life was beginning to look pretty good again!

It looked even better as I realized that the parking lot where we'd settled to rest was completely empty. Maybe the day was just too cold for many people to want to hike. Maybe some big sporting event was happening on TV that they'd all stayed home to watch. Who knows? All I knew was that I didn't have to worry about the horses getting spooked by hikers or their vehicles.

But the empty parking lot meant that it was also quiet. Very quiet. The only sound beyond the occasional creak of shifting saddle leather was the wind soughing through the pines and around the rocks. It was a music only the mountains can produce. For those who don't hear it every day, it's a sound that offers a sense of peace and calm but also a discomforting awareness of being very much alone.

Perhaps that is why I felt so comforted as I dismounted by the reminder that I'd brought my rifle. After tying the geldings to a tree, I unsaddled the one I rode, then unpacked the other before giving both a ration of grain I'd brought along. I propped my saddle on a nearby log, then spread out my saddle blanket on the dirt next to it. Before sitting myself down on this cowboy lazy-chair, I dug some cheese and jerky from a saddlebag and unholstered my .38 caliber rifle. Exactly why I wanted to lay my rifle across my lap as I ate, I cannot say.

Maybe it was because I loved that weapon and just wanted to look at it and feel the smooth polished wood of its stock in my grip. Or maybe it was to help me feel I wasn't altogether alone. Or maybe I just needed it to complete the image I had of myself as a cowboy—or rather, a *desperado*—on an adventure.

For any and perhaps all of these reasons, I loved that rifle. But as I laid it across my lap that afternoon, I couldn't have anticipated that before the day was out, I'd have an even better reason to love it.

He sets my feet upon a rock making my footsteps firm.[2]

Let them be ashamed ... who seek to destroy my life; let them be ...
brought to dishonor who wish me evil.[1]

~

4

DESPERADOS, WHY DON'T YOU COME TO YOUR SENSES?

After finishing my cheese and jerky and taking a long pull of water from my canteen, I finally started to relax, enjoying that peaceful feeling of being truly alone. This was just about as good as life got!

Then I heard a sound in the distance. My two horses perked up their ears too. They were both looking toward a gorge that sloped down the opposite side of the ridge from where we'd come up. At first I couldn't see anything on the trail that had drawn their attention, but I quickly determined this was where the sound I'd heard was coming from. It was some kind of vehicle motor, which was odd since the Forest Service didn't permit motor vehicles of any kind on these trails.

As the horses and I waited, the sound grew louder and drew nearer until I finally spotted an off-road three-wheeler type motorcycle making its way up the gorge trail in our direction. *A weekend warrior*, I mentally dismissed, assuming whoever it was would go on by and my peace would be restored.

But just in case the motor got loud enough to spook the horses, I leaned the rifle against the log where I'd laid my saddle and got to my feet. I then walked over to the horses and began stroking their necks to keep them calm until the cyclist passed by.

The trouble was, he didn't!

When the three-wheeler finally emerged at the top of the trailhead about fifty yards away, the first thing I noticed was its rider sizing up my horses and me before coming to a full stop. For a few long seconds, he just stared at me, then turned around to take in that the parking lot was empty. As he returned his gaze toward us, a smile spread across his face, revealing what seemed to be a missing tooth.

Curious, I thought. Then I noticed a large dog emerging beside the three-wheeler. It appeared to be the result of some German Shepherd's romance with a black Collie, its dark mottled longish hair mangy and matted on a wolf-like frame. Where had it come from? I hadn't seen it coming up the trail with the three-wheeler. But it was quite clear as the mangy mongrel rested on its hind legs, tongue dripping and panting for air, that the man beside it on the three-wheeler was its master.

The only thing I could figure was that the dog must have taken a different route up the mountain to join him. But that left the question of how the dog's master had brought such a formidably large dog up the mountain in the first place. It was too big to have ridden all the way up from the lowlands on that three-wheeler. Maybe the guy had a pickup parked somewhere else. Who knew? But then I thought, who cared? It wasn't my problem.

Of greater concern was what the dog's owner might be thinking behind his smile as he continued to stare at me.

The man's next move was to rev his cycle and start rolling it slowly in my direction, the dog trotting after him. When he got close, he turned his engine off and rolled to a stop about ten feet from where I stood with the horses.

Even before he stood up, I could tell he was a big man, probably in his late twenties, a little over six feet tall, and around two hundred and ten pounds. Much like his dog, the beard and long hair emerging from beneath a cowboy hat was scraggly, dirty, greasy, and in some places matted. Besides blue jeans and boots, all he wore was a too-small open leather vest and red bandanna, which did nothing to cover his well-muscled naked torso. I clearly needed to work out more often!

And that was before he got off his three-wheeler. When he stood up, I noticed that he also had a denim shirt tied around his waist in such a way that almost concealed a holster containing what I immediately recognized as a .357 Magnum handgun. Altogether, his bearing was not of a man remotely safe for a guy like me—or for that matter, anyone—to be alone with on a remote mountaintop.

His smile widened as he headed my way, verifying that he really was missing a front tooth. "You mind if I sit with you a minute?"

"Why?" was the response that popped into my mind. It wasn't as though we'd likely have a lot in common to talk about. Of course, I didn't say that out loud. But he was already settling himself on the ground next to his dog so his query was evidently of a rhetorical nature. Then, leaning back against one of the tires of his three-wheeler, he began to talk, a conversation that lasted for well beyond one very long hour.

Like any conversation with a stranger, we stuck at first to generalities like the beauty of the forest, the majesty of the mountains, and the virtues of getting away from the maddening crowds down below in the cities. Once we reached the weather, the conversation trailed off, and it seemed we'd run out of topics. But just when I was thinking this was wrapping up and he might move on, he nodded toward my rifle. "So why are you carrying that?"

That was when an already cool conversation turned downright chilly.

I first told him I carried it for rabbits, snakes, and perhaps an occasional coyote. But he kept staring at it, so I began nervously telling him more about the rifle and the reasons I liked it. He acted like he'd never heard of a .38 rifle, so that's when I grabbed the opportunity to reach for my rifle while offering to let him see one of the bullets. This let me lever the action twice to eject a cartridge he could inspect while leaving another in place in the chamber. As I tossed him the ejected bullet with one hand, my other hand returned the rifle to my lap, where I intended to leave it for as long as it took for this guy and his dog to leave.

I was comforted by the fact that the rifle was ready to fire—and even more that we both knew it. Of course this left the unspoken equation lingering just beyond the realm of our seemingly idle conversation. Could I cock my rifle's hammer and pull the trigger faster than he could draw and fire his .357 Magnum? To say the least, an interesting question. Hopefully, he was agreeing with my math that had the odds tilting in my favor.

My new companion was no longer smiling when he looked up from the bullet I'd tossed him, but I saw an almost imperceptible twitch on one side of his face come and go in a blink. The question with which he broke the pregnant lull my object lesson had left in the conversation suggested his mind was indeed doing the math.

"So maybe you're also carrying that rifle in case you run into some bad hombres up here?"

That's when I really wished I'd taken some acting classes. Notwithstanding my dad's prohibition as to that particular career path, it would have been nice about then to be able to persuasively pretend I wasn't a bit concerned about this man's possible intentions to do me harm, if not do me in.

Trying my best to project the impression his question hadn't set off alarm bells in my brain, I answered as casually as I could muster, "Not really. I hadn't thought of it."

I paused before continuing, "But now that you mention it, that's not such a bad idea. I guess you never know who you could come across in a place like this, do you?"

He nodded agreement and stretched his lips into a smile that displayed his missing tooth. But his already narrowed gaze morphed into something a lot more like the cold, glassy stare of a rattlesnake. At that point I figured I had little to lose so we might as well acknowledge the elephant in the room we'd both been ignoring.

"Is that why you're carrying a pistol?" I asked.

He nodded again. "Yep. Believe me, I've come across some bad hombres passing through these mountains. You can never be too careful is my motto. I'm never without a gun when I'm up here."

He might have been offering helpful advice, but the look in his eyes told me he was thinking something else. That was when I knew I was stuck. To re-saddle my horse and leave, I'd have to lay my rifle down. But the way this conversation was going, I wasn't about to do that as long as he was around, much less let him get behind me without my rifle in hand while I worked on the horses.

So there I sat with little more to say and even fewer options. Nor had he given any sign he intended to leave anytime soon. To make things worse, the sun was getting closer to setting. Once that happened, it would soon be too dark to risk attempting the trail to the campground. But I had to because by now my horses were badly in need of water and that was the only place I knew where I could get it.

Yep, I was in a fix.

Then out of nowhere came a glimmer of hope. The sound was much like I'd heard earlier—another engine approaching us from a different direction. I was excited. This could be the help I needed, if only to distract this guy long enough to put the gear back on the horses and get out.

At least that's what I was hoping for. But my hope

turned out to have a short shelf life. My heart dropped into my chest as the guy in front of me waved at a guy now approaching us on a second three-wheeler and called for him to join us. It was quickly evident they not only knew each other, but were friends.

The new arrival was a smaller man with a wiry frame and a filthy derby sitting atop his head. But he was of similar age and also wore a worn leather vest in place of a shirt. Like his friend, he had a holster buckled around his waist that held some type of revolver I couldn't immediately identify.

As he dismounted, he asked the man seated in front of me, "What do we have here, Sundance?"

"Sundance?" I reflexively responded with a bit of a laugh.

They both immediately turned toward me with looks that told me my chuckle at the one man's name had not been appreciated.

"Yeah, that's what I go by," the first man with the .357 said with a challenge in his voice, "Do you have a problem with that?"

"No, not me. I don't care what you call yourself. That's your business," I replied too quickly to hide my awareness that any pretense of our remaining civil was evaporating with each word I muttered.

"Yeah, well. There's a reason," he said, keeping his eyes fixed on me as he gestured toward the other man. "And this is my friend. He goes by the name of Butch. You gonna laugh at that too?"

I thought they had to be joking, so to reduce the

tension in the air I chuckled again and stupidly said, "Butch Cassidy and the Sundance Kid? That's cute."

The trouble was, they didn't laugh with me. Apparently, "cute" was not the word they would have had me use. For what seemed the longest minute of my eighteen-year-old life to that point, they both just stared at me. Fortunately for me, they were the ones who flinched first. With what barely passed for a smile on their faces, they seemed to reluctantly agree that some humor could be found in their newly revealed monikers. But they didn't seem to find anything else funny about the current situation.

And in truth, neither did I, sitting there on a mountaintop with two armed men and no one else within eyesight I could appeal to for help—or maybe even for miles. It didn't really matter what their names were. All I had to know was that the probabilities in my favor had just shifted to them. It was now two to one. If something good didn't happen soon, then something bad would most surely be happening before too long. And that something bad would more likely than not be happening to *me*.

Afforded no acceptable alternative, I continued my "chat" with these two men wearing guns on their hips. Our conversation proved rather captivating—though not the kind of captivating I cared for. By now I was beginning to ask myself the hard questions. Would I be able to shoot these men if it came to that? And if I did, could I get them both before one of them got me too?

Despite my confusion, I was pretty sure I wouldn't shoot either of them even if I could.

A memory came to me of one evening while Papa was

sipping his whiskey when I'd asked why he kept his one gun locked away in the back of his closet. "What if someone broke in one night and you couldn't reach it?"

Without taking his eyes off the sunset, he smiled and gave me an answer I didn't expect. "Son, that's exactly why I keep my gun where I can't easily get to it. I don't want to have to live with shooting a man in any fit of emotion over which I may have little or no control. I'd rather he shoot me, whoever he is, and let him have to sort it all out with God, not me."

"Why?" was all I could think to ask.

With a faraway look crossing his wrinkled face, he responded, "Back when I was young, I almost killed a man in a fit of rage. He had insulted my wife, and in the heat of the moment I thought he deserved to be shot. The only reason I didn't was because by the time I'd gone inside to grab my gun and came back outside to shoot him, he'd already run off. I still cringe when I think of what I would have done if he hadn't. I know I would have shot him.

"Ever since then I still have nightmares from time to time about what that would have done to the rest of my life, not to mention to the lives of my wife and my children, if I had killed that man. All to say, I decided long ago never to put myself in a position like that again. After all, think about it, Son. Had I actually killed that man, you and I would probably not be sitting here right now enjoying this beautiful sunset, would we? I could still be in prison, and you might never have been born. Give that some thought."

After that evening I can't say how much thought I gave it. But one thing was sure. His words came back to me that afternoon on that mountain as I found myself nursing a frail conversation with my two new "friends" that seemed likely to peter out to nothing pretty soon.

"What would Papa do?" I thought.

I was pretty sure I knew the answer to that so I went a step further. "What should I do?"

Looking at those two guys seated in front of me, I really didn't have an answer. Nor was I sure if it was my reason or my emotions that was driving this mental roller-coaster that had raised all these questions in the first place. Which in turn left me silently praying to the God my grandfather worshipped to give me the right solution.

"God, please help me! Please, God, help me!" echoed in my head.

In the core of my being, I knew then that I really didn't want to have to decide whether or not to shoot these men even if they pushed it that far. Entirely lost on me at the time was the irony that not many hours earlier I'd been praising the same God to whom I was now pleading for help because of our successful traversing of a washed-out trail. That earlier experience seemed like nothing compared to this twist of circumstances in which I now found myself trapped.

That was when I once again heard the sound of an engine motor. But this one was very different from the other two I'd heard earlier. It was much louder and emitted what could only be described as a thunderous, thumping cadence that did not seem in any way familiar in our immediate surroundings but most certainly sounded ominous. Now what?

The horses were responding to the noise by dancing around and pulling on their reins. Even the two armed hombres had clambered to their feet and looked concerned. The thunderous cadence rose to a roar as it approached ever closer from the direction of a gorge that sloped down toward the flatlands.

Then we all saw what was making the noise as a helicopter literally climbed up into view. It paused, hovering no more than a hundred feet above where we were sitting. Looking up, I could see the pilot, and he no doubt could see the three of us.

Butch was the first to identify the aircraft as a sheriff's helicopter. He quickly took matters into his own hands (excuse the pun) by raising both hands toward the helicopter to give it a double-barreled middle finger salute. As he did so, he was yelling at the top of his lungs the very epithet that in my opinion his salute had already conveyed quite effectively to those in the helicopter.

I guessed that told me all I needed to know about Butch's sentiments on that particular subject. Sundance, less than pleased by his compadre's behavior, yelled at him to sit down and shut up. Perhaps he wanted to avoid what I was desperately hoping for—that the sheriff might decide to come down and join our conversation.

Regardless of our different views, I think all three of us were surprised when the helicopter paused beyond the ridge, then suddenly made a tight U-turn to land perhaps fifty feet away in the very parking lot in which we were sitting. Dust stirred up by the chopper was blowing everywhere. I now felt safe enough to set my rifle down and turn around to calm the horses.

As the helicopter's engine thundered, armed deputies all wearing the same green uniforms poured out of it to form a huddle beside the aircraft. They seemed to be waiting for the pilot, who was still talking to someone over his mike.

My horses were moving restlessly, but also blocked any view the officers might have of me. My mind started racing in panic mode, and for some unknown reason all I could think of was that I needed to unload my weapon. I didn't want them to approach me and find a loaded weapon. But I also didn't want them leaving before I could talk to them about helping me get out of there and far away from these guys named Butch and Sundance.

Reflexively, I grabbed the rifle and started levering the remaining bullets out as rapidly as I could. The noise from the chopper and the officers' various radios covered the sound. Only later did I come to fully appreciate how incredibly stupid I'd been to do this. Who knows what might have been the case had any of those officers happened to see me cocking my gun!

In any event, I had finished and was leaning over to pick up the bullets I'd ejected when I was stopped by the sight of Forest Service and law enforcement vehicles that seemed to pull into the parking lot from every direction. As personnel emerged from the vehicles, they all spread out and suddenly displayed weapons that were pointed directly at the three of us. Then they started to yell.

"Stay down!"

"Stay seated!"

"Don't move!"

"Stay where you are!"

"Keep your hands where we can see them!"

Needless to say, Butch, Sundance, and I all froze. I let my beloved rifle drop to the ground without giving it so much as a thought. I could hear Sundance angrily whispering to Butch, "You're such an %#&!. Now, look what you did?"

"I didn't do this. This isn't my fault. Don't blame me, you %#&!," Butch growled in response.

"Just shut the %#&! up and don't do anything else stupid!" Sundance continued in an angry whisper, "They got nothing on us. We'll be fine. Just let me do the talking."

Then one of the officers, who had been cautiously sidling our way, pistol in hand, shouted another order. "Slowly place your hands behind your heads, lock your fingers together, and keep them there."

Once all three of us had complied, he continued, "Now, keeping your hands locked where they are, lie down flat and roll over very slowly on to your stomachs. Don't move your hands away from the back of your heads for even a second. Understood? Now, do it!"

Another officer quickly collected our firearms while others started body searches to look for more weapons and extract our wallets. To their credit, it took only a few questions about my horses, my dad's ranch below, and calling in to headquarters about my student I.D., which I had on me, to determine I was not with either Sundance or Butch.

An officer soon told me I could stand up and start

saddling my horses. I immediately grabbed the opportunity. But I cringed when—much as Sundance had asked earlier—one of the deputies asked, "Why the rifle?"

"In case of rattlesnakes," I answered, then couldn't help adding, "Or you never know. Maybe also for self-defense in case I crossed the path of any bad guys?'"

I could tell the officer didn't like my answer. But in light of the two hombres still lying flat on the ground, he couldn't very well disagree with me. Instead, he told me to take my horses and move along. As they say in the movies, I was free to go. And never was I happier to be able to do so.

With the sunlight now quickly dwindling, I saddled and loaded my gear on the horses with no waste of time. I was mounted up by the time two deputies had finished hand-cuffing both Butch and Sundance.

As I turned my horse to leave, I'll never forget the look on Sundance's face when he looked up at me from the ground and asked, "But what about my dog? Hey, mister, can you help me out? Take my dog, and if you give me your address, I'll come by and get him when they let me out."

Incredulity joined my relief and urgent desire to get out of there. He had to be kidding! What kind of a request was that? Nor was I about to let him know where I lived.

Kicking my horse to start him moving, I said over my shoulder, "Sorry, Sundance. I can't help you."

About an hour later, the darkness of that evening finally descended as I set up camp a couple miles away at the campground that was completely deserted except for my horses and me. My mind and emotions were still reeling over all that had happened since I'd met Sundance and Butch. I had my tent set up, the horses fed and watered, and my dinner on a campfire when one of the forest rangers who had been part of the raid drove into the campground and pulled up by my fire.

"Are you okay?" he asked.

I told him I was, then asked if he could tell me why Butch and Sundance had been arrested. His response didn't surprise me but left me feeling even more fortunate than I had earlier. Blessed, in fact, by the way things turned out.

Butch and Sundance had been on a wanted list by both the Forest Service and law enforcement for several months. They'd allegedly knocked off a number of liquor stores and other businesses at gunpoint in various small towns along the perimeter of these mountains. But since they disappeared into the mountains after each robbery, they'd successfully eluded arrest for some time. Apparently, they'd taken to hiding out in various abandoned shacks scattered throughout the forest along trails like the one I'd seen Sundance come up earlier in the day.

Unfortunately for them, the day they'd chosen to visit with me on the ridge was the first time they'd been out in the open long enough for a Forest Service ranger driving by on the dirt road that ran along the rim to spot them and coordinate their arrest with the sheriff's deputies who'd arrived by helicopter. In short, I had unknowingly served to distract these two bad guys long enough for their crime spree to be brought to an end.

After relating all this, the Forest Service ranger asked, "So what were you guys talking about all that time?"

"Everything, yet nothing really significant," I answered. "I just knew I wasn't comfortable putting the rifle aside to load the horses. The only reason we talked as long as we did was because I couldn't leave. Until the cavalry arrived, I really had no other options available."

Smiling, the ranger looked up into what by then was a night sky. "Well, I guess you really should count your lucky stars tonight. Because those guys were some *bad* guys, and what you were today was lucky. Very lucky!"

Papa had once told me something else that didn't make as much sense at the time he said it as it did that night. "Son, there is no such thing as luck. God knows everything. So when you're in trouble or going through a trial in life, give the problem to God and then don't take it back. Just stand back and watch. He'll not only help you through it, but most likely it will be in some way you would not have imagined possible. He writes better scripts on how things will play out than we could ever dream up. And in time you'll also come to learn he's got a great sense of humor."

I thought of Papa's wisdom that night. Did God use me to help stop Butch and Sundance from hurting somebody else? Did God answer my prayer begging him to help me? Was he the one who helped me not have to shoot them? Not to mention, not be shot myself? Was God the one who arranged for a helicopter full of deputies to simply appear in the middle of nowhere to rescue me from the trouble he saw me in? Did God use Butch flipping them the double-barreled bird to let the pilot of that helicopter know where he needed to land?

Perhaps.

At any rate, looking up at the stars that night, I sure thought so. Those millions of stars can be seen in their full splendor only in the wild, and that night they were out in spades. Their brilliance was so amazing that instead of thanking my lucky stars, I found myself thanking their Creator—for the second time that day. God had indeed given me an adventure I'd have loved to tell Papa about, and at the end of my prayer I tacked on a request for God to be sure to give Papa a hug when he next got the chance.

But all those thoughts about God disappeared just as quickly as they'd come as I headed downhill the next morning to return to the "real" world. I honestly gave God little further serious thought in many of the years that followed. He played at best a minor supporting role in the unfolding theatrical production of my life, and I called him to center stage only as a last resort when the narrative left me no better alternative than to talk to him.

I am just grateful today that God didn't dismiss me from his mind as quickly or easily as I had dismissed him coming down off that mountain.

The heavens are telling of ... the work of his hands.[2]

I ... discerned among the youths a young man lacking sense.[1]

❧

5

RUN JANE RUN, SEE JANE RUN

Mini-skirts were still the rage when the women weren't wearing hip-hugging bell-bottom blue jeans and tie-dyed tank tops without bras. We guys wore much the same, but the tightness around the hips and lack of bra was less a social statement than it was for the women.

As we sauntered to and from classes in our sandals of choice, trying to look cool, we pondered serious matters that had little to do with what we were in school to study. Such as the need for global citizens like ourselves to find solutions for things like war, famine, and disease that our parents had obviously overlooked. After all, the times in which we were living were far more serious than our parents' era—unless you counted WWII—thanks to the war in Vietnam, the military draft, and all the anti-war protests and other civil unrest sprouting up around our campus as they were throughout the nation.

While my siblings and I were growing up, my parents made sure we attended church weekly, though they couldn't ensure we actually listened to the sermons. Now that I was living in a college dormitory many miles from home, I considered myself free to choose my own path.

Looking back now, I recognize that while I did believe in God when I left home for college, this was less any real personal belief than part of my job description as the son of my parents and grandson of my grandparents. You could say—except in situations like my mountaintop encounter with Butch and Sundance—that my faith had the depth of cellophane. It was there but so thin you could easily miss seeing it.

So when I arrived at the university, it didn't bother me much to find I'd forgotten to pack my Bible. And I soon found out by way of practice that *not going to church* could become as much a habit as my prior habit of *going to church*.

It's not that I ever left God out of the picture entirely. Nor do I mean to say that he ever left me. But if my life up to this point were viewed through the lens of a Monopoly game, God was like my personal "Get Out of Jail Free" card. A resource I kept in my hip pocket to be used only when I absolutely needed it. Like the ten or fifteen minutes before every final exam.

The unmitigated effrontery of considering myself entitled to tilt the powers of God entirely in my favor whenever I deemed it necessary totally escaped my attention. Also lost on me was that under this convenient arrangement I was essentially designating myself to be the god of my God.

Oh, the vagaries of youth! In one sense, it's a blessing. Later in life, it makes you appreciate all the more God's inexplicable willingness to forgive us for the all things we come up with that must deeply grieve him when we do them.

In my defense, there were many things to distract the mind of a young man or woman from such weighty thoughts—like the almost full-time job of just growing up and becoming the adults all of us were pretty sure we already were.

For instance, along the main walkway from the dormitory where I lived to the campus at large, I could almost always count on being offered a sermon of sorts by a gentleman who went by the name of Swami-X. Just listening to him made me feel I had become a grownup.

This Swami was a sixty or so year-old stoner with a long gray beard that spilled down from a very weathered face over a bare chest so skinny it resembled a rack of ribs. He would perch himself on whatever inverted crate he'd managed to snag that particular morning in order to stand above the passing crowd. As his skinny arms flailed around above our heads, he would regale us about the virtues of having sex while stoned on weed, then go on to condemn us for our voluntary participation in the *brainwashing* our parents—i.e., the Establishment—called higher education.

It was a distillation of mutilated "wisdom" that left many of us wondering how anyone could get any more adult than to be honored by such a man so willing to treat us as his equal by sharing such "enlightenment" with us. Granted, the basket at his feet made evident his willingness to share his acquired knowledge was less about enlightening us than in hopes that we'd toss a few coins into the basket.

But the knowing look on his grizzled face suggested his possession of some hidden universal "truths" as he stabbed his index finger at those of us gathered around and proclaimed in a stage whisper such intellectual pearls as:

"%#&! the Establishment."

"They want to do it to you. So I say do it to them first!"

"Are you shocked by the word %#&!? Yeah, I can tell you are. It's written all over your %#&! faces. It's because your parents told you it was *a bad* word. Well, I say %#&! your parents!"

"They don't like the word %#&! because they don't want you young %#&! to like sex as much as I do. And that's because if you're getting as much sex as I am, you won't be pissed off enough to want to go to some %#&! foreign land to kill people you don't even know like your parents want you to do. So %#&! them! And %#&! YOU! You're nothing but wannabe Establishment puppets-in-training!"

Then with the grand gesture of a bow coupled with a broad sweep of his arm—presumably to include all within hearing—he'd conclude with, "Thank you all for attending today's lecture. It's been my honor to be able to inform all you %#&!s about America's true need to %#&! the Establishment!'"

That wasn't to say he was done for the day. It was just his way of letting us know he was going on break—probably to crawl into the nearby bushes to take a leak. After his break, he'd return to continue on pretty much all morning of each day school was in session. Based on his scrawny appearance that was far more akin to a skid-row wannabe than a 21st century Don Juan, few of us believed he was actually leaving us to get laid. But it was clear one way or another that the Swami didn't care much for working afternoons or weekends—or for that matter, what we thought.

As to his talking points, to our know-it-all young ears, Swami-X probably kind of already knew he was basically preaching to the choir. Which didn't mean we weren't often entertained by his bold and sometimes hilarious demonstration of what the Constitution meant by our unalienable rights to assemble and speak freely within the public square. If our generation of college students could be characterized by anything, it was:

- A frequent recourse to weed.
- A blind belief in the short-sighted notion that *free sex* really could be "free" of any longstanding harmful consequences.
- A general antipathy even before we encountered the Swami's "pearls of wisdom" toward a war many considered belonged to "the Establishment."

In short, the Swami wasn't telling us much we didn't already think we knew but simply served to confirm, if not reaffirm, the "veracity" of our generation's newly discovered "wisdom."

Speaking of the Vietnam war, my draft number was

92, and by that point in 1971-72, student deferments were on the wane if available at all. In fact, I recall being informed by the aggregate student body wisdom making its way through the halls of my dormitory that all draft numbers under 120 were pretty much guaranteed to be going to "Nam."

With 92 being a number considerably under 120, I soon joined others in developing a keen interest as to what guys like President Nixon and his buddies were thinking of doing with guys like me. As in things that could get me killed in a war that didn't seem to be going too well for anybody on any level.

Not until twenty-four years later would Secretary of Defense Robert McNamara finally admit in his 1995 memoirs that the Vietnam War itself had been "a mistake" and that his escalation of that war was in his belated words, "wrong, terribly wrong." For all those—like me— whose lives his *mistake* had put on the line by 1971-72, his belated confession of error was a tad too late to make any difference. Even more so for the countless who had already died for that "mistake." All to say, guys like McNamara might have done the nation a favor had they listened more attentively, if not thoughtfully, to guys like Swami-X.

For the rest of us just trying to get to class on time, our encounters with the Swami left us with a host of reactions to a war many already knew was a mistake long before the Swami told us and became even more sure of it long before McNamara finally admitted it.

At one end of the spectrum were endless debates in the dorms and around campus about things like the meaning of patriotism, the pros and cons of capitalism vs. communism, and the legitimacy of the *domino theory*, which was the argument that if communism wasn't stopped quickly in a place like Nam, it would spread around the globe like cancer, eventually leading to America's demise.

To our young brains, this was heady stuff, but many of us felt up to the challenge. We would argue the finer points of such global matters into the wee hours of the morning, lubricating our intellect with our choice of beer or wine or for those true disciples of the Swami—which, let me make clear, I was not—of weed. All of which served little purpose other than to leave us feeling like elite members of a higher and enlightened social order that resided on firmer moral ground than our elders—not to mention extremely exhausted the next day.

At the other end of the spectrum were actual protesters of the war. These were those willing to take to the streets to promote their convictions in the public arena via acts of civil disobedience. By the time I got to college, such protests had amped up in terms of tension and potential violence to a degree that couldn't be—and wasn't—ignored by either dorm "intellectuals" like me or the Establishment.

The shooting of protesters by the Ohio National Guard at Kent State had occurred just a year or so before this. So going to one of these protests had become something of a high-risk decision for anyone whom the authorities might perceive to be a member of the anti-Establishment, anti-war, anti-draft "rabble." Both arrests and beatings were very foreseeable consequences, at least for those with fully formed cerebral cortices. Which, as has been noted, many of us did not yet possess.

Perhaps that is why my dad called me at my dormitory one night to talk about the protests occurring on my campus and to order me in no uncertain terms never to attend such an event. I can admit that even back then I thought this was advice well worth taking. Even my undeveloped cortex knew that getting arrested with a broken head would not be a good thing.

As Dad put it to me: "Once they start flying, neither a bullet nor a billy club is going to give a gnat's whisker about the finer nuances of anyone's political insights. So you stay away from anywhere they might be flying. Even if you're not guilty of anything, the danger just by virtue of being there can be very real. Got me?"

"Got ya, Dad. Okey-dokey."

"Don't you dare 'okey-dokey' me! I'm dead serious about this. You got me?"

"Sorry, Dad. I didn't mean okey-dokey. I got your message, and I'll stay away from trouble."

"Good, Son, that's better. Talk to you later."

Like I said, this made sense even to my young mind. And as a rule I did mostly stay away from such events. But there are always exceptions to any rule. And for me two events in particular taught me that the dangers of just being present at such protests were, like my dad said, very real.

The first time was when Jane Fonda and her second husband—the radical anti-war activist, Tom Hayden— came to speak at our university. Apparently, they wanted to talk to us about the evils of the war. It wasn't that I was a fan of theirs or their ideologies. But they were famous—or at least she was. Besides, their scheduled appearance was just a short walk from my dorm.

What could it hurt? I thought. After all, I wouldn't be in the crowd. I'd find a place somewhere off in the distance and stay safe even by my dad's standards. It would all be good, no?

As it turned out, "no" was most certainly the answer to that query!

I'd chosen a spot far above the protesting multitudes for my role as spectator in this Fonda/Hayden theater of the absurd. The men's gymnasium was located off to one side of a grassy area that surrounded a platform where the couple would be speaking. After taking the elevator to the third floor of the gym, I climbed a final flight of stairs that took me to the roof.

From my perch, I could see everything without being part of the crowd that was there to protest. Pure genius! Even my dad would have been satisfied. Or so I thought as Jane and Mr. Hayden took to the improvised stage that had been set up by who knows who and the crowd of almost a thousand students down below me welcomed them with enthusiastic applause and cheers.

In the beginning, I have to admit it was exciting. Hayden's opening speech was not much different in form and substance than that of the Swami standing on his box a couple hundred yards down the way. But Hayden was a lot more famous—or should I say, infamous—than the Swami as one of the defendants in the Chicago Seven trial, which involved seven—originally eight—anti-Vietnam War protestors being charged by the federal government with conspiracy, inciting to riot, and other offenses related to protests during the 1968 Democratic National Convention in Chicago, Illinois.

His wife was even more famous, not only because Jane Fonda was the daughter of a movie star and a star in her own right, but because her over-the-top sexy "Barbarella" poster hung in virtually every male's university dormitory room in America at that time—right next to Raquel Welch's iconic poster from the movie "One Million Years B.C." Consequently, the voltage of energy and enthusiasm among the crowd surrounding the platform was far higher than anything ever seen at any Swami anti-war debriefing.

But it wasn't long before I heard a cadence in Jane's speech that hadn't appeared in her husband's and never in the Swami's. It was similar to the cadence of a coach attempting to rev up his team before the start of a game or during half-time when the team is behind and hoping to catch up in the second half.

That day the opposing team went by the name of ROTC, an acronym for the Reserve Officer Training Corp that operated on our campus. The ROTC's overall function was to recruit "officers in training" for the military from among students desperately wanting to avoid the draft, since those who signed up were automatically granted a draft deferment that allowed them to graduate before having to serve.

To Jane Fonda, the ROTC was a tumor symbolic of the Establishment's war effort that had been allowed to metastasize in our hallowed university. In her view, this tumor had to be removed, and it became quickly apparent she wasn't satisfied to have it removed eventually. She wanted it removed that day, if necessary by radical procedures up to and including violence.

Even a brain in my state of arrested development could take the hint that this was her intent when she picked up a megaphone and started calling for the crowd to join her in the chant, "Burn ROTC now! Burn ROTC now!"

The crowd was soon chanting—or I should say, roaring—in unison with her. This had an electrifying effect on not only the crowd but my nervous system. I knew I should leave, but I couldn't bring myself to do so just yet. About that time, events started happening in such rapid-fire succession that the "nice outing" I'd only intended to observe from afar transformed into a display of anarchy that quickly became very serious indeed.

As the crowd's chant about burning the ROTC intensified, I saw Jane hand the megaphone to some guy I hadn't seen before. He continued the chant without skipping a beat as he walked around the perimeter of the crowd to the far side opposite the platform. Still chanting, the crowd turned to follow the sound of his voice on the megaphone. This left them now facing the opposite direction from where Jane and Tom remained standing on the platform.

That was when I noticed the police in riot gear who had lined up behind the crowd, which had now turned to face them. I looked back at the platform, wondering what Jane and Tom were planning next. They had disappeared from view. Where were they? Had they joined the crowd they had amped up?

I couldn't spot them in the mob below. And before long I no longer cared as other issues had become more pressing. Like the police, who were now inserting themselves between the chanting throng and the building on which I stood. Why had they moved there?

Who cared! All I knew was I needed to be somewhere other than where I was at that moment.

I was looking around to figure out my options for a speedy and safe exit when I saw something I'll never forget. At some distance from what was now the back of the crowd, Jane and Tom had taken advantage of the cover offered by a heavily landscaped path to slip away from the lawn where the student protesters continued to chant. I watched with a sense of betrayal as they clambered into a waiting limousine, which whisked them from the anarchy they had just instigated.

Even to a protest rookie like me, this did not look good and in fact left me with a rather poor impression of them both, notwithstanding my favorable opinion of Jane's Barbarella poster. Then my attention was drawn away by a somewhat more significant factoid that had just dawned on me with all the subtlety of a thunderbolt of lightning. The ROTC offices the crowd wanted to burn were located on the ground floor of the very building from which I was watching. Wasn't that just super!

"Burn ROTC now!" suddenly took on a whole new meaning that for me had now become very personal. I had to get out of there—and fast in case some of the protestors made it past the police and succeeded in their appointed mission to burn the building to the ground.

Fortunately, I could see from my rooftop vantage point that the action was contained so far to the north side of the building facing the lawn area where the speeches had been held. After bolting down various sets of stairs that took me to the ground floor, I found an exit that allowed me to escape out the south side of the building.

There I quickly merged with other college pedestrian traffic that for all appearances remained oblivious to Jane's and Tom's recent antics of anarchy. It was almost surreal. The sun shone and students walked casually back and forth past the Swami, who was still lecturing off in the distance as though this was just one more day of school.

From there, I headed back to the dorm for dinner as if nothing had happened. As my racing heart began to still, I told myself, *Wow, that was close! I should have listened to my dad. Maybe God was using him to tell me something.*

But that was then, and these thoughts didn't linger in my mind for very long afterward.

Deliver my soul.... from lying lips, from a deceitful tongue.[2]

Incline your ear to me, rescue me quickly.[1]

6

A SPECTATOR'S PERIL

Anti-war protests on or around campus seemed to be happening with increased frequency as we moved into 1972. The good news was that Nixon seemed sincere in his intent to bring the war to a close. The bad news was that my draft number came up that year, which strongly suggested a combat tour in Nam could very well lie in my future.

This was also the year Jane Fonda made her infamous visit to Hanoi shortly after urging the rest of us back home to burn down the ROTC offices on our campus. Who knows? Maybe she left the country thinking she needed a vacation after learning that it never did go down in flames. Whether that was because of the police intervention, or because the ROTC happened to be in a brick building that she and I both failed to realize wouldn't burn so easily is anybody's guess. Go figure! On to the next protest.

One thing for sure is that Jane's hijinks in North Vietnam definitely raised the subject of *treason* in our late-night dorm debates. The flip side of that same coin was that her actions and those of others like her seemed to embolden other protesters at schools like mine to step forward and publicly speak what they firmly believed was their truth to those in power.

It was all pretty intoxicating stuff that was occupying rent-free more of the space between our ears than our pea-brains could afford. The result was a lot of confusion with many on both sides of the war argument feeling they had a lock on a truth that even today remains elusive.

Perhaps this is one reason why one day several hundred students at my school decided it would be a good idea to protest the war by taking over the school's administration building. The school administrators and police strongly disagreed as to this being such a good idea, but that didn't seem to stop anyone.

A number of young adults entered the building, interfering with the work of employees and asking them to leave. To my knowledge, nobody lawfully in the building was injured in the process of being removed by protesters, but they were all forced to leave.

Other protestors surrounded the building, blocking the entrances and engaging in what by then had come to be known as a "sit-in." Burning draft cards and the like also helped pass the time between speeches—read *rants*—being given by anybody with access to a hand-held megaphone.

The theoretical point of bringing "business as usual" to a halt at the school seemed to be a vain hope that somebody far, far away in Washington, D.C. would be told about it and agree forthwith to end the war. Few of the protesters were likely too optimistic their efforts would have that effect any time soon. But even if it didn't bring the war to a close that day, for many it presented a fun and emotionally fulfilling way to spend the afternoon.

It wasn't long after this particular sit-in began that the press and police arrived en masse at the scene. Consequently, news of what was being referred to as a "happening" spread across the campus like a wildfire being blown by a strong headwind. Given all this, I must ask, how could any normal person—like me—not want to go see what all the excitement was about?

After my experience with Jane Fonda several months earlier, I did approach the area of the sit-in with what I considered much greater caution. From a safe distance across a vast grass quad, I could see several hundred students milling around the administration building. So far, so good.

Even at this distance, I could hear the official-sounding voice of a policeman on a blow horn informing the protesters of the obvious—that what they were doing was unlawful and that they needed to leave immediately. Presumably, they were all to just go home and do something like—I don't know, watch T.V. or read a book?

Of course, telling protesters to leave is like telling a bunch of alcoholics to go home when the bartender has just announced that all drinks that day are on the house. The police pronouncements only served to make official the excitement these students were already feeling about being exactly where they were and doing precisely what they were doing. They weren't about to leave.

Then again, neither were the police. And, therein lies the rub.

Such was the recipe for what promised to be an interesting afternoon of action and adventure for all concerned —like me—regardless of which side of the argument you happened to fall. In response to my curiosity, I couldn't resist moving forward through an alleyway several buildings from the sit-in. This opened onto a winding street that fronted the entire eastern perimeter of the campus, which I knew would offer a better view of the police response to the current upheaval at the administration building.

What I saw when I emerged from between two buildings shocked me. As far as I could see from one end of the street to the other, dozens, if not hundreds, of helmeted police in riot gear stood shoulder-to-shoulder in lines two and three deep. Their face shields were in the down position, and their billy clubs were held out at the ready. Behind them, a whole host of paddy wagons—i.e., police vans—were lined up with engines revving.

In short, a lot of cops. And they meant business. It was obvious these guys were not going to be fooling around once they were given their marching orders.

Even so, I can remember to this day thinking that somehow I was okay because I wasn't actually involved in the protest. In other words, I can remember exactly how stupid and naïve I was to even be thinking like that.

Then I heard the officer in command shout out into his own megaphone what sounded like the start of a countdown. "Anybody who has not dispersed in *five* minutes will be subject to immediate arrest!"

That's when I made the decision to return to my initial "safe space" and regain the distance from which I'd started my surveillance. As I scurried back between the buildings and re-merged onto the vast expanse of the quad area, I could hear the officer's countdown continue.

"Anybody who has not dispersed in four minutes!"

"In three minutes!"

"Two!"

By the time the bullhorn announced *one minute*, I considered that I'd applied more than an abundance of caution would dictate for me to comply with the order to disperse. Of course full compliance would have involved just going home to the dorm. But that was beyond the limits of what my youthful curiosity would permit.

Not wanting to miss out on this "moment in history," I compromised by electing to get off the lawn area of the huge quad and enter a nearby building in which I often had classes. Interestingly, if not ironically, this was the building used mostly by students interested in *social studies*, which is exactly what I thought I was there to do that day. The building was a safe distance from the administration building but conveniently had windows in each lecture hall that would allow me to see the probable path of retreat most protesters would have to take if those columns of police officers in combat gear actually started heading west across campus with their billy clubs.

Which they did precisely sixty seconds after the officer with the blow horn had given his final countdown of one minute.

To say this police march for all practical purposes

ended the students' sit-in experience for the day would be an extraordinary understatement. The chaos that resulted was immediate. Which is to say that when the police began their methodical lockstep march toward the administration building, the students and any other protesters who weren't already standing immediately jumped to their feet and started running, screaming, and yelling. At first in every direction, but they soon herded up, the center of their mass heading mostly west across the grass quad away from the advancing police. This placed the retreating mob on a collision course with the building where I'd planted myself to look out the window of an empty second-floor class-room to observe the event.

Men and women seated just moments earlier in protest of a war were now doing their best to keep a safe distance from the line of approaching policemen. Many were walking backward as they retreated so they could face the police, flipping them an occasional "bird" as they screamed Swami-X-like epithets at the "pigs." Others were throwing anything they could find handy at the officers. Still others, wrapped up in the anger of the moment, got too close and were hit with billy clubs, which were swung with a force seemingly equal to what Babe Ruth might have used to slam one out of the park.

To my mind, those struck by such blows were sadly misguided unfortunates who should have known better. In the adrenaline-charged atmosphere of that day, they had only too clearly ended up with the short end of the genetic stick when it came to choosing between their fight or flight impulse. I can't remember if it was a class in biology or psychology where I'd heard such a highly charged environment produces the fight or flight instinct in the amygdala gland located in the frontal lobe of the human brain. But some of those guys on the ground would have benefitted significantly had they also attended that lecture and listened with more considerable attention, if only to avoid getting their amygdalas smacked that day.

The impact of the billy clubs caused most of these social warriors—male and female—to immediately crumple to the ground. They would then be grabbed by other officers and dragged off in the direction of a paddy wagon crawling along behind the advancing officers. It wasn't pretty.

What eventually happened to these warriors, I do not know. From what I saw that day, some were very obviously bleeding and otherwise appeared to be seriously injured. Rumors flew in the days that followed of broken bones, broken skulls, and in some cases permanent brain and spinal damage. But nobody seemed to know for sure. Perhaps even more disturbing, it wasn't long after the protest was over that nobody seemed to care about those they probably would never see again. As with most casualties of war, those who never really knew them soon wrote them off.

It wasn't long before the lines of police had crossed the grass quad and were passing directly below the window in which I—thinking I was kind of like the invisible man—thought I was safely perched. That is until I heard someone yell, "%#&! YOU PIGS!" from the window located directly below mine.

In and of itself, that crudely dismissive declaration would hardly be worth mentioning in context of all that was happening—and being shouted by others—within my range of view. Its significance comes from the fact that the epithet was followed almost simultaneously by a powerful blast of water from a fire hose shooting out of the same window below me. I watched with horror as this hostile yet non-lethal expression of protest knocked four or five officers completely off their feet.

Of greater concern were other nearby officers who now turned their focus toward the assailant. As a group, they rushed toward the entrance of the building. My first thought was that the future of the guy below me didn't look bright if the police caught up to him.

Then an awful brainwave occurred to me. What if they didn't get a good look at the water canon operator and made the mistake of thinking I was the guy who did it?

Oh no, this is not good! I told myself frantically.

The police might even just arrest everybody in the building to sort it all out later. That most certainly would include me. How could I ever hope to explain this to my dad? I had to get out of there. But to where?

Heart pounding in my chest, I ran desperately out of the empty classroom and into an equally empty hallway. Floating up a nearby stairwell were the echoed shouts and movements of officers storming into the building on the floor below me. I knew immediately that going down the stairs was not an option. This left just one other.

I bounded up the stairs by as many steps per lurch as I could manage, then headed up to the third floor. The hallway was once again empty when I arrived, but I could hear the thud-thud of an officer's boots coming up the stairs below me. Unless I did something fast to disappear, in my mind I could see them soon tackling me to the floor.

All I could think to do was run toward a door with some professor's name printed on it to see if it would open. Fortunately, it did. In fact, there sat the professor himself working at his desk as if nothing outside his office mattered. Funny how that works!

As I rushed through the door and closed it behind me, I looked at him with my heart pounding in my throat. He looked up, and I can still remember the complete calm with which he asked, "What's going on? Is there a problem?"

I explained hurriedly why police were searching the building. Without the slightest shift in his calm expression, he asked, "You're not the guy they're looking for, are you?"

"NO!"

"Very well, then. Have a seat. So far as anyone's concerned, you and I have been working on a very important project of mine for most of the day."

I thanked him as I took a seat. Then we waited. It wasn't long before the professor's door opened. A policeman with an adrenaline-induced snarl on his reddened, sweaty face asked who we were and what we were doing there. I let the professor do all the talking and just hoped the officer wouldn't notice the sweat on my forehead.

Fortunately, the police officer took the professor's word that we were working on something. Once the door closed behind the officer, the professor whispered for me to wait where I was until all the police had left the building. Then he gave me directions to a rear exit he said would leave me in a cul-de-sac behind the building we were in that wasn't likely to be crowded by either police or the protestors.

We said our goodbyes. Regretfully, I never crossed paths with him again, but that's not to say I haven't thought about him with deep gratitude many times over the years. As I left his office that day, pouring out my appreciation for what he'd done, he interrupted with a smile, telling me to get while the getting was good. I didn't need to be told twice.

Realistically, if that were true, I wouldn't have found myself in trouble that day, would I?

In any event, once beyond the cul-de-sac I crawled downhill under cover of the landscape only to find myself on the same path down by the school gym that Jane Fonda and Tom Hayden had used to make their escape several months before. As I reached the lower level of campus, I could see smoke from tires that had been set ablaze to impede the progress of the police. By the time they could get around to dealing with the blaze, I intended to be long gone and eating dinner back up at the dorms.

And indeed I was.

Close call? Yes.

Had I been warned? Yes. Once by my dad and once by my experience with Tom and Jane.

Had I heeded these warnings? No.

Would I do it again? Not wanting to press my *luck*, I certainly hoped not.

Six months later, I no longer had to worry about attending any more draft protests because there wouldn't be any. That's when, thanks to President Nixon, the military draft was brought to an end, freeing me to go on to law school.

At the time I thought, *am I on a lucky streak or what?* But as before, I was completely ignoring the flip side of that question:

If it wasn't luck, what was it?

He caused the storm to be still.[2]

With flattering lips and with a double heart they speak.[1]

~

7

AN INVITATION I COULDN'T REFUSE

Now that I was freed from the threat of the war, the rest of my college years passed by like a cool breeze. Sadly, along with the Swami, it all soon became only a fond memory placed into the file of my past.

Perhaps sadder still was the fact that as I prepared to go on to law school, I still had no appreciation for the possibility of any *miracles* having come to pass that had allowed me to get this far. But one good thing I would come to know is that if God is anything, he is patient—and he knew I had more to learn.

During this period, my parents were doing what they could to also help me find a wife other than the girl I was dating at the time. So it shouldn't have surprised me much that a month before my graduation from college, upon learning that my girlfriend and I had broken up, my parents announced that they'd arranged an invitation for me to go on a cattle drive down on my grandmother's family ranch. This was on the ranch of some relatives of my dad's whom the family had kept in touch with over the years. Country cousins, you might say.

You may be wondering if they were related to my paternal grandmother's relatives who had shaken their heads when she and her family took off for L.A. decades earlier, saying, "They'll be back." If so, the answer is yes.

So off I went the summer after graduation to drive a real herd of cattle I was told would be comprised of more than just one cow. How could I say no? This would fulfill all my fantasies about being a real cowboy I'd nursed during those summers I spent with Papa on my family's "ranch."

Our job on this cattle drive turned out to be moving three or four hundred cows fifteen or twenty miles from their winter pasture to the one where they would spend the summer. That didn't sound too tough. On the first morning, I was up at five a.m., boots on and first in line to get the bacon, eggs, and heart-stopping biscuits and gravy being loaded on the table for breakfast.

I didn't appreciate until later that how much I ate of such country breakfast fodder would have directly proportional intestinal consequences during the next fourteen hours I'd be bouncing around in a saddle. But I was there to live and learn, and live and learn I did.

Among other things I learned was that cattle didn't gather easily. And when they were gathered they didn't move anywhere very quickly. By the end of that first day, I realized this adventure in total was going to take three or four very long days. Which meant going from before sunup until sundown with just a few breaks for eating or to let the cows rest from time to time.

Since everybody else on the trip had done this before, by default I was assigned to the rear of the herd, where most of the dust they kicked up as well as the pods of prairie poop they dropped along the way were to be encountered. That didn't bother me. I actually found it fascinating to watch dozens of cow sphincters periodically processing cow biscuits throughout the day. It was akin to observing a huge non-stop pasta processor. Only in this instance it was being served as a dish that had the appearance of a thickened pesto sauce.

The back of the herd was also where calves that got separated from their mothers would cut and try to run back to the last place they'd seen their mothers, which could be all the way back to where we'd started that day. The first time this happened, I watched as the calf's trot away from the herd broke into a run. Then I heard my dad's country cousin yell to me, "Get him!"

It wasn't so much a suggestion as an order. But I was glad to accommodate. Upon spinning my horse around, I quickly discovered it knew from experience what this was about far more than I did. The athletic quarter horse gelding I rode was in excellent shape and took off after the calf with a speed I'd never before experienced.

What I didn't know was that calves can outrun horses in a head-to-head race. So the direct approach of outrunning them to get out in front often failed. So it was this time. Even though my horse was traveling at such a speed I found it difficult to keep my boots in the stirrups, I was still losing ground to the calf

Fortunately, one of the cowboys helping on the drive was well aware of this factor and came to my assistance. Coming in from somewhere off to the side of my trajectory, he was able to cut the calf off. Having stopped the calf's stampede of one, he then stewarded it back to the herd to find its mama, chuckling to himself as he passed by me with a wink.

I for one was just glad to have stayed in the saddle during the high-speed rush of it all. So I hardly noticed the good-natured ribbing throughout the rest of the day from all the cowboys who had either witnessed the event or heard about it from others who had. If they got a good laugh out of it, I was just glad to be of service.

The only other event of note came on the last day of the drive when we had to cross the railroad tracks paralleling the far side of the highway that separated the winter and summer pastures. I'd heard them all talking about it but didn't appreciate why it was such a matter of concern until it actually came to pass.

To a cow, train tracks are similar in appearance to the cattle guards used at gateways to keep cattle confined. For this reason, cattle don't like crossing them, and when forced to do so, they are easily spooked. Well, that's what happened when we did it. Without warning, the entire herd broke into a charge, and we had a full-blown stampede on our hands that had to be stopped before the several hundred cows scattered and disappeared into the tall mesquite bushes that lay beyond us.

Obviously, I'd never experienced a stampede before, and there I was in the middle of one. I'd been heading north when the cows decided to bolt to the south. I reined my horse around to get into the flow of things. But the horse took this to mean I intended to charge, so charge he did. As he spun, a tall mesquite was in the way. Instead of going around, he chose to jump it. I didn't get a vote in the matter. Jumping over the bush took us several feet into the air just as I was still trying to recover my balance from the initial turn south.

The result? We landed on the other side of the mesquite, my horse intent upon keeping up with the cows quickly notching it up to full speed ahead and me barely hanging on. In short order, I was watching the sprinting cows from under my horse's lurching neck as I barely held on trying to get back up in the saddle. I literally had one boot in a stirrup and the back of my other heel clinging to the seat of the saddle near the pommel as I hung off on the side of the charging gelding.

Fortunately, I reflexively grabbed the pommel with one hand and in short order was able to pull myself back up into the saddle, but not before I saw my life pass before my eyes. Had I lost my grip and fallen off, I have little doubt my boot caught in the one stirrup would have resulted in being dragged to death under the pounding hoofs of a horse that seemed committed to getting to the front of the charging herd.

Eventually, the stampede was brought to a halt, and the cattle drive concluded by the end of that day. All in all, it was a great experience clearly punctuated with moments of excitement. Aside from the heat, dust, and two blisters I'd developed on my rear end from long days in the saddle, I thoroughly enjoyed it.

That said, I should add that had I been able to foresee then how that trip would redirect the trajectory of my life, I would never have gone. But that is a matter to be taken up elsewhere.

For now, it is enough to know that the local custom among ranchers was to share the load for cattle drives, branding, and the like when more help was needed than they could afford to hire. That's how I met the daughter of a nearby ranching family who showed up each day to help us move the cows. Apparently my dad's cousin had mentioned to him that she might be joining to help with the drive. For my folks this was an added incentive to send me on the trip.

The young woman was a shapely cowgirl in her early to mid-twenties whom I found intriguing when viewed through all the cattle dust and the fog of my hormonally-driven brain. All that to say, I couldn't help but notice that in the midst of all those cows she was the best thing to look at. She often rode near the rear of the herd where I was, but not near enough to suit me. Even so, by the end of the cattle drive we were both of the opinion that our infrequent encounters over the last several days of riding trail had been a good thing. So before I left, I invited her to visit me in California and she accepted.

From there the whole thing got out of control and took on a life of its own. Mainly because my parents were ecstatic about the possibilities, and so were hers.

Her parents saw it as a solution to a daughter who in their world was already approaching old-maidhood. In other words, she was already a few years past the age of eighteen, by which time her culture strongly suggested she should have already started a family.

For my parents, it presented an end to the drama my college girlfriend had occasioned them for some time.

The upshot was that we both quickly found ourselves on the receiving end of incredible family pressure from both sides to make sure the possible match worked out and became *permanent*.

By the end of her trip to California, I found myself engaged, which made just about everybody happy—except me. Yes, I obviously found it hard to resist everybody's endorsement of the idea. But today I can admit that doubts in my mind still lingered at the time and caused me some degree of anguish.

Those doubts were shoved aside when she suggested I call my future father-in-law to ask his permission to marry his daughter. He asked me about my timetable for the marriage. He must have sensed my reservations when I responded, "A year from now would be good. I'm going to law school in the fall and would like to marry your daughter after I complete the first year."

To me, this sounded reasonable. And truthfully, my answer was also an attempt to resist the momentum that had formed to cement this union as well as to put the brakes on this emotion-driven roller coaster I was riding that had gotten so out of control.

But my future father-in-law wasn't having it. The tone

of his reply sounded like I'd insulted him. "Well, if that's what you want. But it doesn't sound to me like you're all too eager to see this through to the end. Are you sure you're serious?"

Stupidly, I took up the challenge he seemed to be laying down. "Well, then, when would *you* want it to happen?"

To which he asked, "When's your school start?"

"September."

"How about we set it for August then?"

"You mean *before* I start law school?"

"Yep."

"That's only two months away!"

"Yep."

And, that's when I caved. Not wanting to lose face in front of him, much less his daughter, who was sitting two feet away listening to the call, I responded, "Well, sir, if that's what you want, then that's when it'll be."

"Sounds good to me. Talk to you soon, son." He hung up, leaving me to wonder what had just happened.

Bad negotiations on my end, that's what happened!

That is how I came to marry my future ex-wife, whom I barely knew and who barely knew me. Neither of us knew for sure whether we loved each other beyond everybody in both of our worlds telling us we should. The only thing we really knew was that we were expected to love each other just because her family knew my family and had been close friends for many years long before either of us were born.

Or at least so they said. A point that even today

remains up for debate, I was to find out later. I only wish Papa had still been alive back then. Perhaps if I could have talked to him, he would have been able to give me a better insight into the lay of the land I was entering. But then who knows? He might have been as excited as everyone else. Then again, knowing most of the players as well as he did, maybe not!

By the time I graduated from law school in Chicago, we'd already had our first child. I was excited to move on and get a career going. At least in my mind, I thought having a law degree offered us a world that would be nothing less than a grab bag full of opportunities out there just waiting to be, well, grabbed! Surely, that would make my wife happier than she'd seemed throughout our years in law school.

Unlike college, the three years I spent studying law had been arduous, to say the least. My wife never seemed quite happy, but I'd attributed that to homesickness. In time she would get past it. Especially now that we had an infant son to keep her occupied while I attended class and hid out in the library to study.

As to the enterprise of learning the law, perhaps that experience can be summed up best in this way. Imagine a group of people who have been the best of the best in their studies since birth. And ever since their days in high school, everybody who they thought counted—not to mention their moms and dads—had reinforced in their minds repeatedly and often the notion that they were *absolutely brilliant.* Then bring together two or three hundred of such people—who, by the way, completely believed all they had been told about themselves—from all around the country and put them in one class at a top law school to compete against each other as to who really is top dog.

This leaves you with an institutional cauldron in which, by invitation only, one experiences three years of purified group narcissism on steroids.

Suffice it to say, when I finished law school I was glad to be moving on and excited to head back to the west coast to join a premier law firm in Los Angeles as what partners in the legal field called a *first-year associate*. That is a newly minted attorney who has just passed the bar exam following graduation from law school and is in his or her first year with the firm. Which really means a *newbie* to the practice of law whom everybody in the law firm knows is a long, long way from ever becoming a partner.

For newbies like me, such finer points were often lost in the emotional rush of it all. Among the things that dazzled me was getting my very own office in a relatively new downtown high rise where people worked who were—I was told—*very important.* I would be high up on the twenty-second floor where like other important attorneys already working there I could look down upon all of those less fortunate souls on the boulevard below. Could life get any better than that?

Little did I know that the answer to that question would soon become—*well, yes, it could.* But that is a matter we will take up soon enough.

Shortly after settling into my new office, I received my

first of many *intra-office memos*. These were informational missives the firm's partners would put out from time to time to inform those associates working below them—err, with them—of some important decision or directive—i.e., edict—that they for whatever reason had decided to issue. These memos would be placed in manila envelopes with flaps bound by string wrapped around circular clasps to give the matters enclosed within the appearance of "confidentiality" and "utter importance."

Needless to say, this was the preferred mode of intraoffice communication in law firms back before laptops, emails, and text messages had even been imagined by people like Gates and Jobs, who were probably still teenagers working in their parents' garage.

The first such official memo I received was directed to all first-year attorneys in the firm's Los Angeles office. As I unwound the string to release the envelope's flap, I saw that it was from a partner I had yet to meet.

How exciting! I told myself. *I wonder what this is about!*

It certainly turned out to be exciting—sort of! The memo was about a dinner party hosted by the firm especially for the firm's newest associates. All first-year associates were therefore invited to attend. I found it interesting that no RSVP was either required or requested. Apparently, any first year's unavailability to attend was NOT an available option. Or so my new secretary, whom I shared with two other first-year associates, informed me.

I soon learned I'd just been initiated into the law firm's culture of "firm-speak"—i.e., the use of select words as polite substitutions for other, shall we say, more awkward words that any reasonable mind would find equally applicable. For example, the use of the word *invited* instead of *ordered* when it soon became apparent what the partners really meant was the latter.

That being realized, appreciated, and understood, and since I didn't want to make any waves, I made the plans necessary for my wife and me to comply with this most kind *invitation*—i.e., *mandate*. The dinner party was to be held in the home of an attorney recently selected for partnership in the firm. What I didn't know at the time was that this new partner had received an *invitation* to be our host from the same senior partner who had issued our own invitations.

In time, I would learn that it behooved the senior partners to put on full display such proverbial *carrots* as the impressive digs of the firm's newest partner to convince newbies to keep on *endeavoring to persevere*. Such carrots would be continuously dangled before new associates throughout their partnership track. This encouraged them to remain willing to be worked to the bone for the ten years it would take to work their way up to eligibility for partnership themselves—should the other partners allow them to make it that far.

That was how we came to be hosted that night by the firm's newest junior partner and his wife Lauren. The senior partners were well aware the couple had just bought their home to celebrate becoming the firm's newest partner, and they wanted the firm's latest recruits to see what they could look forward to with enough time and hard work.

And for the uninitiated like my wife and me, it worked —at least in the beginning.

Let him not trust in emptiness, deceiving himself; for emptiness will be his reward.[2]

A man's pride will bring him low.[1]

❧

8

SOMETIMES GUACAMOLE CAN ROLL UPHILL

As my wife and I approached the party location that night, I couldn't deny the house was beautiful. It was an impressive two-story mansionesque-like dwelling overlooking a golf course in the heart of an affluent neighborhood on the Palos Verdes Peninsula near Los Angeles. What we didn't discover until later was that our hosts hadn't even unpacked in most of the rooms and shouldn't have been expected to entertain that night at all.

We showed up that evening exactly *on time*, which I guess in firm-speak could be translated a bit *too early*. In any event, we were the first to arrive. When our hostess opened the door, I instantly noticed that while Lauren's late-thirty-something face presented a mouth that was smiling, her eyes most certainly were not. It was obvious from the get-go that she wasn't thrilled in the least at having been *invited* to give this party to which we'd been *invited* to attend.

With that understanding firmly in place, I couldn't think of anything to say as my wife and I shook Lauren's hand and accepted her suggestion to come inside. In truth, every fiber of my being wanted to flee. It just didn't seem like it was going to be a very fun affair.

Lauren encouraged us to make ourselves comfortable while she went to "freshen up" before the others arrived. Turning on her heels, she then left us to stand around considerably less than comfortably in her entrance hall until that mission was accomplished.

Upon her return, it was clear Lauren had given some thought about what to do with us until the other guests arrived as she suggested a tour of her new home. Her words were gracious enough, but her tone and expression made it clear she was fulfilling an obligation that gave her no pleasure.

Lacking any better alternative to suggest, we defaulted with, "That sounds great. We'd be thrilled!"

The tour was interesting enough, but what I found myself thinking most about as we traveled through the seven bedrooms of the house was why their dog was so thirsty. For the entirety of the tour, Lauren's huge Labrador retriever followed us from room to room. In every bathroom we passed by, he managed to find the toilet and loudly lapped up a drink with his slobbering tongue.

I was well aware that dogs often do this, but I have to say it was becoming amusing how many toilet bowls were so employed by the dog in the course of our journey. *Well, if it doesn't bother Lauren, who am I to care? But, really, every toilet in the house? What's with that?*

Eventually, Lauren, the dog, my wife, and I had made a

full circle and returned to where we'd started. There we encountered Lauren's rent-a-maid, who in our absence had set out appetizers all around the living-room that opened up to one side of the entryway.

It was an array that included the usual suspects — sliced vegetables, cheeses, and nuts alongside a variety of chips and dips. But what made this particular offering of appetizers uniquely attractive was the centerpiece that had been placed on a large coffee table. This was a massive mound of guacamole set in ice that was literally the size of an inflatable beach ball. It was indeed a beautiful piece of culinary artwork, and I for one couldn't wait to give it a try.

That is, right up to the moment when Lauren's big drooling Lab sauntered over and began lapping away at the beach ball with his still-dripping tongue that minutes earlier had been repeatedly used as his own personal toilet ladle. Somehow, that changed my mood about the whole food experience I'd been anticipating.

Who knew dogs liked guacamole?

Maybe Lauren?

But let me back up a moment. When Lauren saw what was about to happen, she screamed. But before she could grab the dog's collar, it had already slurped a huge hole in the side of her mountain of guac. To her credit, she at first appeared both shocked and saddened, as I certainly was. But her remorse, unlike mine, was brief.

Mind you, no other guests had yet arrived when the guac attack occurred. So Lauren made a calculated judgment that absolutely discounted my wife and me being actual witnesses in the room. Exhibiting a bark of her own, she ordered the maid to take hold of the Lab's collar and dispatch the dog to the back yard. She then grabbed a large spoon off the coffee table and proceeded to fill in and smooth over the hole in the guac—dog slobber and all!

Also to her credit, I must say she did an admirable job. When she finished, it was impossible to detect that the hole her dog had just made had ever existed. Her party was back on track, and she clearly presumed a tacit understanding that my wife and I would remain silent about her extreme remedy to rectify the canine damage we'd just witnessed. After all, who were we to her? At best, we were the new kids on the block she obviously considered irrelevant and perhaps even expendable should we ever betray her trust. So it was that without a word said all currently present in the room—including Lauren's maid—entered into our mutual pact of silence.

In short order, the other first-year associates started arriving and began to fill the room. None had started eating anything, much less the guacamole. This reluctance was probably in polite deference to the senior partners, whom we were told would be there soon. The avocado beach ball was just too pretty to touch before the VIPs were present.

As promised, the senior partners soon arrived with their wives and Lauren's husband in tow. After that, I could do little more than be amused by the events that quickly unfolded.

To kick the evening into motion, Lauren had begun introducing the various new associates to the senior partners —since many would not yet have met all the partners. She now seemed to be into the swing of the party. But she would soon find out her position at center-stage was to be short-lived.

One of the senior partner's wives had been standing nearby listening to Lauren. For our purpose in this narrative and the sake of irony, we'll call her Prudence. Evidently compelled to put into proper relief her position of superiority as wife of a partner far more senior than Lauren's husband, she abruptly interrupted her hostess's introductions.

Prudence started her uncomfortable segue with a seemingly generous commentary on the beauty of Lauren's new home. But she ended her compliment with a conversational stiletto placed squarely into our hostess's back, commenting loudly enough for all to hear how surprised she was that Lauren and her husband had moved so quickly to this house after her husband's promotion.

"Especially in light of the fact that even with a new partner's income it will take some time before you can hope to afford to furnish this place properly and replace all these things you had to bring over from your apartment. Don't get me wrong, dear. These pieces are cute. But eventually you will want better. It will just take some time to do it is all I'm saying."

Ouch! Talk about a conversational dead-end! Prudence's snide comments immediately drew everyone's attention to the worn, second-hand appearance of the furniture presently bearing the weight of Lauren's various and sundry appetizer trays. Her words carried just the right amount of condescension covered with a glaze of pretentious wisdom to suggest that we should all be wondering whether Lauren's furniture pieces would be able to support us for the rest of the evening without collapsing.

Personally, I thought Lauren's furniture looked pretty good. Especially compared to what my wife and I were used to. Thus, I stood there stunned, not quite believing Prudence had actually said what she just did. From the fleeting frozen expression that appeared on Lauren's face, she couldn't either. Even the partners in the room—junior and senior—were left speechless by the plausibly deniable rudeness of Prudence's statement delivered so eloquently under cover of a seemingly appropriate compliment.

It was now game on! Thrown off balance by the abrupt cooling of the atmosphere, all remained silent to see how Lauren would respond. Would she fold? Respond with some snarky rejoinder? Or gracefully pull off an adequately courteous conversational rebound?

I must say, Lauren pulled it off as perfectly as one could under such circumstances. In fact, she pulled out of the emotional nosedive the snarky comment must have caused her with a grace that was actually quite impressive.

Without skipping much of a beat and with supreme poise, she slowly turned toward Prudence and said, "Well, thank you, Prudence. I agree that's probably quite true. And whenever it happens that we can afford more appropriate furniture, I would really hope you would be willing to give me some guidance. Having seen yours, I know with you by my side I couldn't possibly go wrong."

With an artful toss of her head, she returned her attention to the rest of her guests and added with a smile, "Of course, that's a conversation for another time. For now, Prudence, I must insist—no, please, I want you to be the first to render a verdict on my guacamole. It's a special family recipe, and I hope you'll like it."

"I'd be delighted," Prudence responded with a pursed smile that belied her pretended false humility.

With that, Lauren glided into action with all the deference she could muster. "Here then, let me get you a plate."

My wife and I watched with no small amount of amusement as Lauren grabbed the same spoon she had used earlier to smooth over the guacamole. She then proceeded to fill a plate from *exactly* the spot in the mound where a hole had been left earlier by Lauren's slobbering Lab.

Then, with a chillingly frozen and—perhaps only to me—almost sinister smile that I remember to this day, she handed the plate to Prudence, saying, "Before we all dig in, please do us the honor and let us know what you think."

Prudence took the plate from Lauren, smiling in appreciation of the homage she clearly thought she was being given and firmly believed that she deserved. With pomp-and-circumstance, she scooped a chunk of the canine-lubricated guac onto a chip, placed it in her mouth, went through the motions of slowly savoring it as one would a fine wine, then nodded her approval.

At which point, Lauren directed a knowing smile of her own at Prudence before turning back to the rest of us.

"Okay, everybody. Now that Prudence has given us her approval, let's all enjoy it." Gesturing at the food all around us, she added, "Help yourself to anything you like while I pour everyone a drink. Then we'll take a tour of the house before dinner."

This time hopefully, the dog would not be joining the tour. As the saying goes, "guacamole rolls downhill." And most often, that is probably true. But on this day, I learned that how we treat others can sometimes cause it to roll in the opposite direction. Even if as in this case it's tinted green instead of brown. And, if the person at the top of the hill—like Prudence—is not careful, they may never see it coming.

For me, God used Prudence that evening to present a lesson in the importance of humility. Without it, we—like Prudence—can unwittingly make ourselves vulnerable to attacks that not only can blindside us but inflict harms upon us in ways we may never know.

Of course, true humility can only be obtained when a person realizes that without God in our life we are nothing —a lesson I'm pretty sure he may have intended to teach me earlier—first with Butch and Sundance and then later with the professor who saved my bacon that day on campus. But at the party that night, this greater lesson continued to elude me. The only thing I knew for sure was that I sure felt lucky to have had the inside scoop on the guac.

Perhaps that is why God patiently brought me to a dark

neighborhood on a Sunday night to again try to teach me that without him my next stand—like General Custer's—might very well have been my last.

~

The arrogance of your heart has deceived you.
You who live in the ... loftiness of your dwelling place.... from there
I will bring you down.[2]

He ... has done great and awesome things for you, which your eyes have seen. [1]

～

9

CUTTING CORNERS

By the time I was coming into my second year at the Mega-Firm, I had decided to look for less expensive parking.

The reason? My wife and I had our second son, and the money the firm was paying us no longer stretched as far as it had at first. Cheaper parking seemed a smart way to extend my income further toward the end of the month.

I soon found a lot on the other side of a freeway over-pass from where I worked. This was in a lower income residential neighborhood comprised mostly of run-down apartment buildings, small shops, and a liquor store or two. But, hey, the uncovered ground-level lot was half the price for parking as the parking garage beneath the high rise in which I worked, so how bad could it be? Practically speaking, it was only three blocks or so from my office. Since I was young and in good shape, I figured the money saved would be well worth the short walk.

Initially, all seemed to work out well. But I soon learned this was only true during regular business hours on busy weekdays during daylight.

Not long after I'd initiated this clever financial maneuver, I had to work late one Sunday night. Because the sun had set, the parking lot where my car resided was on the dark side of a freeway. By which I mean that there was little illumination from either streetlights or buildings. All of which transformed the area after dark into a place worlds away from the civilized locale in which I worked.

As I approached my car that night, I noted that the only significant light in the area came from a single street lamp hanging by wires above the center of the intersection, which did little to illuminate the corner lot where my car was parked.

I hesitated briefly, but I was tired so started crossing the street to where I thought I'd parked my car. All I wanted was to get in my car and go home. I was thinking of little else until I noticed that something about the car I assumed was mine wasn't as it should be.

That's odd! Maybe I'm looking at the wrong car. Maybe it just looks like mine.

But when I glanced around at a few other cars still in the lot, I saw no others like mine. No, this one had to be mine. Then a sinking feeling settled in my gut. Something was moving inside the car that shouldn't have been.

As I cautiously drew closer, I realized that there were two men in my front seat. Red bandanas wrapped around their heads, they were bent over as though looking at something on my car's dashboard. At first they seemed oblivious to the fact that I was approaching them, though the single street lamp in the center of the empty intersection now shone directly above me.

My next reaction was shocked anger at the wrongness of it all. What were they doing? More importantly, what should I do?

All I could think of was to start yelling things that upon later calm reflection were inane in the circumstances. "Hey, what are you guys doing? Get out of my car!"

I paused. I guess I was expecting them to be ashamed of being caught trying to steal a car. Or at least worried enough about getting arrested to abandon my vehicle. Instead, they raised their heads slowly as if to see who was making all the noise. So I tried again, "What the blankety-blank do you think you're doing in my car?"

I paused again, still hoping my brilliant utterance was sufficient to get them out of my car so I could go home. But they only continued to stare silently at me through my windshield. Clearly, these two guys weren't the sort who could be easily intimidated, much less frightened away.

This left me with no choice. I pulled out my trump card, yelling in as angry a voice as I could muster to disguise my growing fear, "Get out of my car NOW before I call the police!"

To get an idea of how stupid this last statement was, you need only consider that at this time cell phones had yet to be invented. To even attempt making such a call to the police would require first finding a pay phone in that isolated area, then hoping that once I got there I'd have enough change in my pocket to make the call. I'd also have to hope these two guys would have the patience to just sit here and wait for all this to happen. Not likely!

In the panic of that moment, everything I was yelling seemed appropriate enough. After all, surely these guys would surely not stick around with the possibility of police showing up.

I was wrong!

I saw the two men exchange a few words. I couldn't hear them, of course, but I could guess they weren't discussing my continued good health.

Then the front doors on both sides of my car slowly opened. In unison, the two men emerged and shut their doors—or should I say, my doors. With Mona Lisa smiles, they started sauntering toward me, the distance between the two of them widening as they approached.

In the blink of an eye, I knew exactly what a sheep must feel when it realizes two wolves are heading in its direction after having decided what they want for dinner.

The oversized baggy pants riding low on their hips, the red bandanas wrapping their heads, and the chains hanging around their necks and off their wrists told me more about these guys than I wanted to know. Then again, the fact that I couldn't see their hands, which were shoved into the side pockets of their denim jackets, made me want to know more about them than I did. Were they holding knives? Or worse yet, guns?

I had no way of knowing. But the closer they got, I

could tell these were the kind of gang-bangers who might easily have either or both. As I took all this in, I stopped yelling to look around and ask my now-panicking self, *What now?*

There were no police—or at least none I could see. There wasn't even any traffic to speak of, perhaps because it was Sunday night, much less any pedestrians I could call out to for help. Apparently, everybody in this dark neighborhood with a brain—unlike me—was safe in their home getting ready for Monday.

Instinctively, I found myself backing up to stand directly beneath the single streetlamp hanging above the middle of the intersection. My hope was that the brightness there in comparison to everywhere else around me would cause my new friends to reconsider whatever they were planning and stop their slow advance in my direction.

Again, I was wrong.

The distance separating us had narrowed to an alarming few yards, their spread-out tactic signaling their intent to come at me from both sides. Still, I was afraid to leave the pool of light since they could just outrun me and trip me up somewhere out there in the dark. With few options available, all I could think to do was to start yelling inane threats again with the hope they might still be scared away.

But the two men appeared in no way impressed or swayed by my renewed ranting. The knowing squint in their eyes coupled with cruel smiles told me they knew their neighborhood better than I did and that no one was likely to come to my aid before they finished whatever they intended doing with me—or should I say, to me.

I was cooked. And they knew it.

And so it was that I found myself doing once again what I'd done with Butch and Sundance several years before—muttering under my breath a panicked plea to the God of my granddad. "Lord, please help me. Please, God. Don't let this happen!"

Whatever *this* might turn out to be.

Did I offer this prayer with much hope? Honestly, I couldn't say. But about then I sure hoped there was a God who was listening. I also now appreciated why people in foxholes during battle are said to pray the same. In such moments, one realizes it really *is* the only hope one has left. The last option when all else has failed.

And on that Sunday night it was certainly true for me. Suddenly out of my line of sight, I heard the screeching of tires. The calm smugness on the two men's faces, now just a few feet away, abruptly evaporated, replaced by an expression that told me something was changing their plans for me.

They looked at each other without a word. Then, in no more of a hurry than their initial approach toward me, they turned around and started walking away into the darkness of the parking lot. Only then did I feel free to look over my shoulder toward where I'd heard the screech of tires. A yellow cab had entered the intersection and come to a hard brake just a few feet from me.

The cabbie didn't have to ask me twice to get in. As I

took a seat in the back and slammed the door shut, he said, "I saw you from a block away as I was headed toward the bridge to downtown. It looked like you could use a hand. I had to go around the block but got here as quick as I could."

All I could say in response was, "Boy, you got that right and not a minute too soon. Thank you!"

Amazingly, at the time I never thought to put together my own prayer with the cabbie's miraculously convenient appearance at that intersection. From which it necessarily follows that, amidst my adrenaline-driven exhilaration over my narrow escape, I also never gave a thought to thanking God for this most fortunate twist of circumstance.

The cab driver drove me slowly around the block, then returned to the intersection to retrieve my vehicle. As he pulled to a stop beneath the streetlamp under which I'd been standing moments before, I spotted the two gang-bangers slowly climbing the stairs located at the back of the parking lot. We watched until they disappeared into the darkness of another vacant lot above and beyond where I was parked.

"Go see if you can get your car started while I wait," the cabbie said calmly. "Don't assume they're gone. Just get in, get out of here, and go home. And be quick about it."

I needed to hear nothing more. Thanking him, I added a tip that wasn't nearly enough but was every dollar I had on me. We said our goodbyes. Then I ran to get in my car and get out of there.

I found one of the rear passenger side windows shattered, the cinderblock the gang-bangers had used to smash it in left sitting on the back seat. I left it there in my hurry to get inside and start my car. As I drove off, I yelled my thanks once again to the cabbie, who also then drove away, never to cross my path again.

The cold wind coming in through the smashed rear window added to the chill I was already feeling as I drove home. The steering wheel was greasy from the two men's sweat, and the stereo they had apparently been trying to steal rattled as it rolled around on the dashboard, still connected by one wire the two guys had yet to cut.

When I got home, I was still in a daze. After walking into our house, I first told my wife all that had happened, then called the police. I wanted to report the crime before we went to bed and let the police know they could find fingerprints left inside the car by the perpetrators of the crime, whom I could also identify.

But the officer who took the 911 call didn't sound impressed with my account. She only asked, "Are you all right?"

"Yes," I responded, "But if that cab hadn't come by, I doubt I would be. These guys were dangerous and need to be caught. So what about the fingerprints? Do you think we can catch them?"

"Are you serious?" the officer asked incredulously.

"Absolutely!"

"I'm sorry, sir. We simply don't have the resources to send a forensics team to investigate every car break-in."

My remedy?

"Just report it to your insurance company," the officer suggested, "and consider yourself fortunate."

"Fortunate?"

"Yes, sir. From the events you've described, the fact that you weren't seriously injured or even possibly killed was probably a miracle. So just count your blessings. Thank you again for calling to let us know. We'll keep a record of your report. Good night, sir."

I hung up the phone with a lingering notion the officer was probably right about the miracle part. But the notion didn't linger very long. Primarily, I felt violated, abandoned, and as dumb as a pile of bricks. The deductible to replace the stereo and window would cost me far more than I had saved by moving to that parking lot.

Probably the better course would have been for me to thank God for that cabbie's willingness to get involved in a situation that could have ended very ugly. After all, wasn't his being there a miracle even according to a 911 officer?

Or had the cabbie's willingness to help just been my good luck?

Whichever he was, he was at least on par with that crew of deputies in a helicopter who had landed on a mountaintop at just the right time. Not to mention the lone professor in a building being stormed by police with whom I'd crossed paths just when I needed him the most.

Mere coincidences? Perhaps.

But perhaps the better question that probably should have been forming in my mind was just how many coincidences it should take for the next one to stop seeming like just another *mere coincidence*.

With this notion, I'm not trying to be cute.
Just honest.

No evil will befall you…. For he will give his angels charge concerning you, to guard you in all your ways.[2]

Exult in ... tribulations, knowing that tribulation brings about perseverance; and perseverance, proven character; and proven character, hope; and hope does not disappoint.[1]

~

10

MY NEW FAMILY

The pyramid scheme that operates in large law firms is something law schools should be required to warn students about by way of a disclaimer at the inception of their legal training—and *prior* to taking the students' tuition.

It works like this.

Throughout the legal education process, law professors hold out the carrot of landing that job at the Mega-Firm. Typically, these are firms with at least several hundred attorneys and in some cases as many as a thousand or so. Some, if not most, have offices in all major U.S. cities and occasionally in foreign countries as well.

Such firms are basically corporate operations where you are told that if you are smart and work hard enough, you can eventually become a revered member of your community. As a byproduct, you will also become filthy rich, live in a mansion, drive the right cars, and be invited to all the important social events.

It would be far more honest and transparent for law schools to require all students to view the entire *Hunger Games* movie trilogy with the advisement that these Mega-Firm jobs we were all working so hard to obtain were not without remarkably strong similarities to that fictional dystopian survival competition.

Such was my own experience in what I came to designate as the *Partnership Games*. Becoming a partner was the ultimate prize awarded to those able to survive the game. But to get there, each combatant had to outcompete their fellow associates since it was a given that not all who joined in the games would achieve that objective by the end of what these firms called their *partnership track*.

Each year, such firms recruit a sizeable number of law school seniors to become their next class of first-year associates—i.e., combatants. The partnership track entailed the number of years—typically a full decade—those associates would have to fight it out before being eligible for even a nomination to become a partner.

Two remaining facts pertinent to these games were never officially discussed. One was that each year the firm —i.e., partners—systematically eliminated a number of associates from each class so that those who progressed to the next level (year) were fewer in number. Thus the inherent pyramid structure of these firms.

The second fact was that promotion to partner was not assured for even those few fortunate enough to survive the partnership track all the way to the end, thus arriving at the top of the pyramid. These still had to be voted on by all the existing partners to determine if they would be allowed to join the ranks of the firm's grand pooh-bahs— i.e., partners. In fact, it wasn't unusual for some senior associates at that level to not make it for one reason or another.

Those associates who didn't survive the vote were usually offered a one-time opportunity to try again the next year. Or they could leave immediately for greener pastures. If those associates who chose to remain and try again didn't succeed the second time, the firm would quietly thank them for their many years of service, then tender to them the *opportunity* to find a job elsewhere. Which this time they did not have the option to refuse.

My first-year class at the Mega-Firm was comprised of sixty-two associates fresh out of law school. In the beginning, we were told that *hard work* was the only ethic that ruled all. If we did enough of it well enough, all would work out just fine.

Or so they wanted us to believe. But few of us at the commencement of our ten-year partnership track were fully cognizant of the fact that the partners had no intention of allowing more than one or two of the sixty-two of us to survive long enough to even be voted on to make partner. Regardless of their work ethic, the rest would be afforded only two options. They could find a way to escape to another suitable job before they were culled. Or they could die—figuratively speaking—in the course of trying to survive the culling process.

As we entered the arena and the games began, we

looked around at the more senior associates already working there and were somewhat comforted by the fact that they all seemed to be educated and seemingly civil human beings. So how bad could it be?

But that was only the perception of the uninitiated. What we couldn't see—because they were no longer around to be seen—were the mortally wounded who had preceded us. Those who had already been removed from the firm's theater of battle and cast aside.

In short, what we were not told was that because of the game's pyramid structure, the isolated, self-contained professional biosphere we had all so gleefully entered was in reality a competition that would be at minimum fierce and oft-times fought without mercy, much less transparency. Greed and ego, being the great motivators that they are, induced most associates to remain engaged in this competition as long as the system would let them, even though it soon became an ordeal for most that in the passage of time far outstripped the pay.

The salaries paid first-year associates were more than most of us fresh out of law school thought we were worth. But what did we have as comparison other than the low-paying student jobs we'd done along the way to get there? Little did we know that the seemingly glorious salaries the firm was willing to pay us would not be tied to any sort of reasonable work schedule that was even remotely proportional to the pay.

Minimum hours to be billed by each associate were officially set by the partners at a reasonable eighteen hundred per year. Even with a two-week paid vacation every year, this comes out to a little less than a forty-hour workweek. So what was the problem here?

First off, there were always some associates with superhuman ambition, tactical abilities, and/or stamina who found ways—sometimes stoked by nefarious and illicit forms of *stimulants*—to far exceed that quota. This of course made the senior partners very happy. So they would find subtle ways to bring to our attention the mega-billable-hours these people produced to encourage the rest of us to get our competitive juices flowing and follow suit. Which we would then try to do to avoid the implicit appearance of falling short by comparison. This was just one means by which partners could increase their *billables*.

Another method employed by partners to achieve the same result was to set deadlines for the associates to complete projects that required tremendous amounts of work to be done in relatively short periods of allotted time. This often necessitated working around the clock and on weekends to meet the partners' demands. Once the project was completed, they would simply assign the associates another project.

The benefit to the partners from keeping associates on this virtual hamster treadmill was two-fold. For one thing, it enabled the partner to look prompt and efficient to the client. But it also gave the partner a mountain of associate billable hours to play with when it came time to bill the client for the work.

That's where an associate's dream of becoming a partner soon morphed into a living nightmare.

From time to time, partners found themselves in the

position of wanting to keep certain clients from screaming about their bills. So any time they thought it "necessary and appropriate" to keep the client happy, they would adjust the bill by cutting from the total a number of hours billed by one or more associates. Unfortunately for the associates whose hours were so cut, this meant some or all of the hours they'd actually spent on the project could just disappear at the partner's whim. And not just from the bill. They would simultaneously disappear from that associate's annual tally of the hours they would be given credit for by the firm.

Moreover, fairness and equity had little to do with these "adjustments." If more than one associate was involved in a project, the hours a partner might cut weren't necessarily taken equally from each associate. Based on the partner's preferences (i.e., favoritism), the hours might all come off the time billed by only one associate, leaving unaffected the billable hours of more preferred associates. What this translated to for the affected associate was that these hours had to be made up on some other project elsewhere by the end of the current calendar year for which the disfavored associate's billables were being tabulated.

So it was that the official eighteen hundred billable hours finish line soon became for many associates an ever more distant mirage they found themselves having to chase. It might seem within view at the beginning of each year, but thanks to the power vested in the partners to effectively keep moving the finish line, it was something extremely difficult to arrive at by the year's end.

In response to such an atmosphere, associates soon

developed their own coping mechanisms. For instance, in anticipation of such "adjustments," it was rumored that some associates would just bill more time for each project they worked on than they'd actually spent. That way if a partner here or there cut their hours, they hoped to come out about even in the end.

Other associates not disposed to so blatantly embezzle money from clients were rumored to do things like finding ways to bill several clients for the same time spent doing some kind of activity. For example, if an attorney had to take a trip to Washington, D.C. for a client, they could bill travel time according to the firm's retainer agreement with that client. But—hypothetically speaking, of course—were an associate able to find a way to link the same trip to the servicing of two or more clients, some could conceivably get away with billing the travel time in its entirety to each of those clients. Was this actually done? I guess you'd have to ask the partners who reviewed the bills to know for sure.

Most associates dealt with the moving billable hour goal post by acceding to the huge-project-with-an-arbitrar-ily-short-deadline treadmill happily offered to them by the partners. In essence, they just worked more and more hours in the hope that even with "adjustments" they would reach the billable hour finish line by year's end. The trouble with this approach was the existence of certain unchangeable limitations that confronted all associates. Like the fixed number of hours in a day. And the fixed number of days in a week.

It wasn't long before associates employing this coping mechanism found themselves pressing up against these immovable barriers and working as close to 24/7 as their health and need for sleep—or the lack thereof—would permit. Their personal lives withered. Pressed shirts were kept in their desk drawers to avoid having to go home. Seventy-two hour stretches at the office without sleep became so frequent as to not be worth even mentioning to other associates—much less any of the partners—in the vain hope of garnering either pity or sympathy. Sooner or later, all were compelled to concede that neither pity nor sympathy for associates having to live this grueling lifestyle was ever available in great supply at such firms.

Not long after the party with Lauren's guacamole-slurping dog that I became educated to the reality that working such hours was a norm for most firm associates. By my second year with the Mega-Firm, my life had become adjusted to the firm-think that this abnormal cultural "norm" should be thought of as normal. After all, it would be worth it in the end once I was a partner with a top-notch real estate practice.

Or so I was led to believe by seeing such things as Lauren's new house. Back in law school when I'd first inter-viewed with this firm, I'd learned that they had over six hundred attorneys practicing many areas of law in six different offices around the United States as well as in London and Tokyo. This horde of attorneys was organized by separating them into numerous *teams.* Each team focused on the practice of different specialty categories within the field of law.

There were venture capital teams, security law teams, litigation teams, corporate/business law teams, tax law teams, employment law teams, trust and estates law teams, banking/finance law teams. And as it turned out, only a single real estate team, a fact the partners who I interviewed with failed to mention when I'd told them this was the team I wanted to be on.

At the time, they'd said my interest in real estate law was not a problem and that I'd be put on that team as soon as there was an opening. What they failed to mention was that my first assignment would be with a venture capital team located in the firm's Los Angeles office, which had nothing to do with real estate. I wasn't informed of this until I arrived at the firm to start work. In the following weeks, I learned that openings on the single real estate law team were rare and highly sought after—primarily by guys like me attempting to escape the abject boredom of some of the other corporate teams they'd been assigned to like venture capital or banking.

To accomplish this feat of getting on the real estate team, I learned that I'd need good reviews from all the partners I was working for in my first year. To that end, I was determined to work my tail off. Which, in fact, I did. And I think I would have made it but for one landmine I inadvertently stepped on.

As mentioned earlier, my second son had arrived on the scene during this first year. Which meant a baby announcement was imperative. For the most part, this was to be mailed to friends and relatives, so I thought little about thanking Jesus Christ for the blessing of the birth in the text of the announcement. I'm not sure that I gave it much thought at all, as it seemed to be a fitting thing for a

Christian family to do. But, as an afterthought, my wife and I decided it would be a good idea to include the members of my venture capital team in the mailing list. I hadn't even considered how some of them might receive the honorable mention we gave to Jesus and really didn't think it would matter one way or the other.

Wrong!

Suffice it to say that it didn't play well in some corners of the firm as certain associates at my same pay grade let me know. One made a point of asking, "What's God have to do with anything? We're lawyers. I certainly wouldn't be broadcasting stuff like that out to the partners if you know what's good for you."

What all of that meant precisely, I wasn't sure. But I decided it was better to not ask and hoped it would just drop right there. Unfortunately, one of the cards had been mailed to the partner I was working for. While he never mentioned receiving it, he also never treated me the same after that. At least that's the only explanation I could find for how the stellar mid-year review I received before the birth of my son morphed into a tepid review by the end of the year without any change in the quality of my work for him.

The short of it was, instead of landing a place on the real estate team for my second year, I found myself landing with a thud on one of the firm's banking teams. What this translated to was an endless sea of documents prepared by other more advanced associates that needed to be reviewed before they were either filed or sent out to clients. It was mind-numbing round-the-clock work, all done under the pressure of deadlines imposed from above by some partner the low-rung associates rarely saw and for clients those associates seldom, if ever, met.

Perhaps that is why one day I finally snapped. Or should I say that I made a conscious *counter-culture* decision to rebel against the "norm" my life had become. I had arrived at the office at 6:30 a.m. By 6:30 p.m. that evening, I decided that for once I was going to just leave and go home at a normal hour.

In firm-speak, that was going home after only a half-day's work, but I didn't care. I just wanted to go home if for no other reason than I was curious to see how much the world outside the firm had changed since I'd last seen it. I also wanted to spend some quality time with my two sons for the first time in ages while they were still awake.

To boost my resolve, my mind first had to try on for size some possible excuses I could give later if anyone asked about my disappearance. Such as, the partner supervising the project I was working on had already left the office by 5:30 p.m., hadn't he? Besides, I could easily pick up in the morning where I'd left off, couldn't I? And our current project wasn't doing anything to literally save lives, was it? If I left now, I shouldn't be missed for a good ten hours overnight, should I?

At any rate, having just come off a seventy-two-hour stint the weekend before, I was willing to take the chance. What I didn't know then was how that decision would become the first step toward freedom from the iron-fisted rule that I'd permitted the Mega-Firm over my life.

I have to admit I was hoping to sneak out of the

building unseen. But such was not in the cards that night. As I waited for the elevator to ascend to the twenty-second floor and whisk me away, a partner from the tax department I knew only remotely came up behind me. With her briefcase in one hand and purse under her other arm, she was obviously calling it a day.

After stepping into the elevator with me, the woman punched the level for the same parking garage to which I was headed. At first we rode down in mutual silence. I nodded, and she nodded back. Then, looking directly at me, she said it—the inferred indictment I had hoped to avoid. "Leaving early?"

What could I say? She'd seen I had my coat on, which was not something an associate would be wearing indoors unless they were leaving to go somewhere—like home. And given our firm's working environment, her underlying assumption that standard working hours for associates extended far beyond 6:30 p.m. was clearly valid. Though it did seem rather hypocritical on her part considering her own utter lack of embarrassment about heading out as well.

Had I been more advanced in my tendency toward professional suicide, I could have responded with something like, "Why do you ask? Are you going to miss the money I could have made you had I worked all night?"

Instead, I tried the only thing I could think of that I felt might float. "Yes, I suppose it is a bit early. But tonight I need to get home to deal with some family issues."

She offered the slightest nod and a thin smile, her tone

almost imperceptibly sarcastic as she responded, "Hmmm . . . well . . . I hope you have a lovely evening."

When we got off the elevator to go to our cars, I bade her goodnight. She walked away without responding. I was never to see her again in what remained of my life at the firm. But that wasn't the end of the conversation she'd started on our trip down the elevator.

When I arrived at the office the next morning, I was still feeling guilty for breaking the firm's unwritten rule about associates leaving early. So when I saw the message light on my phone lit up, I had an immediate cold sinking feeling I must be in trouble.

Once I listened to the message, all doubts were removed. It was from Mr. E. Blotnick, the senior partner supervising the project I was currently assigned to and who had left the office at 5:30 p.m. the night before. The message instructed me to come to his office "whenever" I happened to arrive that morning.

Blotnick was a man in his late fifties who looked like he'd been born in a Brooks Brothers suit. An outward personality like lukewarm oatmeal matched the emotional blandness of his banking practice. But any associate who had worked with him would attest that his gimlet gaze could pierce like knives into a person's heart and soul. Rumored to have been born without a heart of his own, he was the kind of partner who took particular pleasure in the thought of his associates working all night to pile up billable hours for him to play with later while he rested comfortably in his mansion.

Within the firm's banking team that I'd been assigned

to for my second year at the firm, he was not only my immediate boss but the chairman of the firm's banking/finance department. Though by this time I'd worked on his team for nearly a year, I'd had personal contact with him on only a few rare and brief occasions.

He typically handed out the projects I worked on—like proofreading volumes upon volumes of loan documents—through one of the more senior associates who served as his intermediary. Which didn't mean Blotnick didn't retain virtually unlimited power and authority to do whatever he willed with my career and my life.

In summary, while I didn't really know him, I knew enough to have virtual certainty that he couldn't care less about getting to know me in return. So I could only guess why he wanted to see me on this particular morning. I certainly didn't take his request to be a *good* thing. In fact, my paranoia, not to mention my adrenalin, kicked into high gear.

But it was also something I felt would be made worse if I delayed. So I headed off in a hurry to his office. As I passed his somewhat elderly secretary, I paused only long enough to tell her Blotnick had left a message saying he wanted to see me as soon as I could.

Without glancing up, she said, "Yes, he does. Go on in and take a seat. He'll be off the phone in a minute."

My boss had a large, deluxe corner office with an expansive view of the city. Entering, I crossed it as quietly as I could and took a seat facing the desk behind which Blotnick was already seated talking on the phone. As I looked around waiting for him to finish, I took in a certain refinement in his décor that was most definitely missing from the smaller cellblocks-with-a-view assigned to associates like me.

Funny the thoughts that pass through your mind while waiting to be noticed by the person who called you in most likely just to scourge you. I wonder if similar thoughts pass through the minds of those on death row just before *their* execution.

Blotnick soon said his goodbyes to whoever was on the line and hung up. But he continued to ignore my presence, picking up a paper from his desk and reading it for what seemed a lot longer than necessary.

Eventually, he put it down and slowly looked up at me. With those piercing eyes peering over the top of his rimless eyeglasses, I would have preferred he returned his attention back to the paper—or anything other than me, for that matter. From the look on his face, I could tell this wasn't going to go well for me.

"Mr. Nichols," he began. "How's the project you're working on coming along?"

Clinging to the hope of even a pittance of salvation, I replied, "I think well, sir. I should be finished sometime today."

He cut me off and said, "I hope so. Perhaps you did not know this, although I'm fairly certain my instructions had been clear. I was really hoping to have your memorandum on my desk when I got in this morning. But when I arrived, I was instead made to understand that for some reason you had to leave early last night?"

The partner from the tax department at the elevator

the night before! What a RAT! And yet until I also became a partner, there was absolutely nothing I could do about it.

Resigned now to my fate, I demurred. "I did, sir. I had family issues to attend to, and I thought last night would be a good time for that."

"Your family?" he responded.

I smiled, "Yes, sir, personal family business."

He cut me off, putting to me yet again his question, "Your family?"

"Yes, sir."

After a thoughtful pause, he continued, "You're a new associate, aren't you? Relatively speaking."

"Well, actually no, sir. I've been working here for nearly two years. So, I guess you could say I'm not exactly new."

"Well, I would think that after two years you'd have recognized that we at the firm like to think of ourselves as your family, in a manner of speaking. At least, part of your family."

"Sir?"

"We like our associates to feel as though we are all working together like one big family and that your own family is included in that whole. Would you agree?"

"No, sir, I guess I'm not understanding."

"Well then, let me be clear." He paused again. "At this stage of your career and for the future of the 'family' whose business you were attending to last evening, you need to consider seriously the needs of *all* the members of your extended family. That includes *all of us here at the firm.* When you make decisions regarding the needs of your family, you need to prioritize whose needs should be attended to first and given greater import. If you expect to advance your career, then going forward you need to take into account the benefit of all those you should now consider to be your *family*."

Need I say that he wasn't smiling while he finished this seminar on the various meanings one might attribute to the word family? The look on his face was that of someone wondering if what he'd just said had pierced the numbskull of the person he was talking to.

Not wanting to disappoint, I quickly responded, "Yes, sir. I think I get it."

"I'm glad. I'm sure that if you seriously consider what I'm telling you, you will 'get it,' as you put it."

He stood to signal the end of our meeting and said dismissively, "Thank you, Mr. Nichols. I'll look forward to receiving your memo as soon as it becomes available. That's all."

He really didn't need to say that. I think I kind of knew it already. But since he did, I closed out the conversation with the brilliant all-purpose, "Thank you, Sir."

What exactly I was thanking him for, I had no idea. But, really, did it matter?

As I quickly departed his office, I must admit only one word kept coming to mind that had something to do with the south end of a north-bound dog. But I must also confess that by then I'd been so indoctrinated by "firm-think" that I was left uncertain as to whether he was that "south end" or whether it was me for leaving early the night before.

It was a question I pondered and even wrestled with

from time to time over the next several weeks. Little did I know that it would all be resolved sooner than I anticipated. Events were already in the works elsewhere that would give me the answer soon enough.

Consider it all joy ... when you encounter various trials, knowing that the testing of your faith produces endurance. And let endurance have its perfect result, so that you may be perfect and complete, lacking in nothing.[2]

Cursed is the man who trusts in mankind and makes flesh his strength.[1]

~

11

AN OFFER OF HELP POSTPONED

R Nathanson was an eleventh-year associate.

If you recall, the firm's official partnership track was ten years. Nathanson was one of those unfortunates who didn't make the cut the first time around. In the aftermath of the partnership vote in his tenth year, the whispering from the firm's gossip grapevine was that a majority of the partners apparently felt Nathanson lacked the "edge" they were looking for.

Whatever that meant, it was undoubtedly embarrassing for Nathanson. When something like this happened—and as I've mentioned, it happened more frequently than one would like to think—it left associates like Nathanson with only two options. He could either quit and go elsewhere. Or he could stay on for one last try at the end of his eleventh year.

One of Nathanson's classmates, an insurance defense litigator, had already quit some months before when confronted with the same dilemma. In his case, some of the partners he had worked for over the years had met with him to explain the adverse outcome of the vote. It seemed the partners just didn't feel the firm needed another insurance defense litigation partner.

On his way out the door, the classmate closed out by proffering the following question, "Then why the %#&! did you guys encourage me to spend ten years of my life to become one?!?"

A reasonable question given the circumstances and one that resounded in the minds of all the associates he left behind.

Apparently what the partners told Nathanson was more palatable since he'd chosen to stay. But that was not the only reason he'd decided to endure the embarrassment of trying one more time. For eight of the last ten years, Nathanson had been cruising on autopilot under the protective wing of none other than E. Blotnick, who prior to the vote had been sure Nathanson's elevation to partner was in the bag. So when his fellow partners rejected his favored protégé, Blotnick took it personally. Thus it was he who had persuaded Nathanson to stay the course and endure another year. Presumably in that time he could help Nathanson obtain the "edge" the other partners were looking to see.

Nathanson was a nice enough guy. He had a great wife, three beautiful children, and had gone to all the right schools. But like Blotnick, he was bland. For an associate, that could be both an attribute and a detriment.

As a member of the banking/finance team, his personality fit perfectly the incredibly dull and tedious work involved— endless drafting and review of bond agreements and other forms of loan documentation, which was then compiled into numerous volumes the size of thick phone books. This attribute might have helped him avoid being caught up in the swirl of any firm controversies. At the same time, such mind-numbing work rarely allowed an associate to become noticed around the proverbial water-cooler as someone who could even remotely be referred to as a super-star. That laudatory designation was reserved for whichever litigator had managed to achieve the most recent big-dollar settlement or jury award. But that super-star designation was precisely what Nathanson needed at this juncture, and Blotnick was determined to do what he could to make it happen.

The strategy they adopted included moving Nathanson away from under Blotnick's protective wing to give him the appearance of being an independent dealmaker in his own right. So near the beginning of Nathanson's eleventh year, he and his family—life-long California residents—up and moved from Los Angeles to New York to enable Nathanson to take up residence in the firm's office there.

To further burnish Nathanson's bona fides as a brilliant and competent work-horse independently generating mega-dollars in fees the firm just couldn't live without, Blotnick made sure that Nathanson was fed via fax, wire, mail, and telephone all the work he had been doing in L.A. and much, much more. In short, Blotnick knew how the game was played, and he intended to both play it and win —not so much for Nathanson's sake as his own.

Unfortunately, it turned out to be much more work

than Nathanson could handle well. About three weeks after Blotnick had defined for me the meaning of the word *family,* I showed up at work on a bright, sunny summer day. I was pretty sure Blotnick was long past my having gone home early one night. Better still, he was out of the country for the next week networking with some wealthy client. All leaving me with the feeling that life was currently pretty good.

Then the phone rang. One of the secretaries assigned to Blotnick's banking team was calling to let me know that Blotnick had asked her to give me a rush assignment of great import as soon as I arrived at the office. All my feelings that had been so warm and fuzzy just a moment before started to wither.

For one thing, this secretary was *not* Blotnick's secretary, but one who had worked for Nathanson before he left for the New York office. Why would Blotnick use her to convey his message and not his own secretary? Something wasn't right, though I couldn't put my finger on precisely what it was. Could it be that Nathanson himself was using the imprimatur of Blotnick's name to give this assignment the proper color of authority?

"It would be easier," Nathanson's former secretary went on, "if I just swing by your office to show you the project in question rather than trying to explain it on the phone."

"O.K.," I said agreeable while thinking inwardly, *What now?*

The secretary who showed up a few minutes later was a young, fairly inexperienced woman. Upon her arrival, she started in about how Blotnick had left her the message because she'd been involved in the transaction at issue with Blotnick and another attorney in New York I might know. Then she began mumbling about the three-hour time differential and Blotnick thinking it would be most efficient if she were to explain the project to me personally rather than my having to wait to talk to him or the other attorney directly.

That should have been my second clue something fishy was going on since the only attorney I could think of in New York that both Blotnick and I would know was Nathanson, and the three-hour time differential only meant he should be about to go to lunch. So why couldn't he talk? And Blotnick was with clients in Mexico, so his location was in my same time zone. But I didn't push the point any further since this secretary was only the message bearer.

"What does the project entail?" I asked.

"You'll see in a minute," she said without a smile. "If you'll just follow me."

The sense of something fishy increased as I followed her through the long hall and down the elevator to the next floor below, then down another long hallway. Meanwhile, she was gabbing on about something I couldn't understand about Eurobonds I'd not yet dealt with and multiple parties I'd never heard of and hundreds of millions of dollars that most certainly wasn't mine.

She stopped suddenly in front of an office door. "Here it is."

As she pushed the door open, I saw stack upon stack

upon stack of bound volumes of documents that filled the entire room except for a small desk stacked with even more documents. In some cases, the stacks reached all the way to the ceiling. I'd like to think any associate with a lesser amount of internal fortitude would have fainted at the mere sight of it all.

"Here what is?" I asked, striving for a poker face to give cover to a mind already spinning with dread.

"This is your project." The secretary smiled for the first time that morning, but her raised eyebrows indicated her awareness this was no ordinary task I'd been given, but a hose job. I was getting royally screwed by somebody, and she knew it.

"So what exactly does Blotnick want me to do with all this stuff?" I said in a tone that let her know I knew a screw job trap when I saw one.

"These are all the docs for a Euro-Bond transaction for one of Mr. Blotnick's clients in Mexico. Rob Nathanson and his associates in New York did most of the heavy lifting to put this together, then shipped it here for Blotnick's approval. There are over thirty lending institutions involved, each with a separate set of documentation to reflect their individual participation. They have all been promised their correct documentation by tomorrow. So Mr. Blotnick would like you to get it all organized, packed, and shipped by 5:00 p.m. this evening for overnight delivery to the respective creditors in Europe and the client in Mexico."

I was flabbergasted. "Why couldn't they just have a paralegal or secretary do that?"

She shrugged. "From what I was told, each participant has negotiated different loan amounts, terms, and conditions, which will need an actual attorney to sort it all out correctly."

"Are the docs at least organized separately according to each individual participant?" I asked with little hope.

The secretary had the grace to look sheepish. "I don't think so. Worse yet, Blotnick wants you to make sure the exhibits in each volume are attached to the correct loan agreements. There are also loose documents in some of those boxes that need to be included where appropriate."

"Do you at least have a composite list of participants so I have some way to start organizing this mess?" I demanded sarcastically.

She stopped trying to hide her embarrassment. "No, but I've put in a call to Mr. Nathanson asking for that, and we should have it when he gets back from lunch."

"Great! So if this was Nathanson's project, why didn't they ship these docs to the clients from New York?"

"Well, I guess Nathanson wanted Mr. Blotnick to look them over and give his approval. But Mr. Blotnick hasn't had time, and now it's weeks overdue. The clients are getting understandably nervous and upset the documentation for their loans hasn't been shipped yet. Blotnick says he trusts Nathanson, so he wants you to just go ahead and get the docs organized and out the door."

She turned to leave as though attempting an escape before I could ask anything else. But I got in one last question. "Hey, before you go, how did I get picked for this delightful piece of work?"

"I don't know for sure. Something about your needing the hours to catch up?"

After she closed the door, I sat down among the towering stacks to contemplate the project while I waited for her to return with the list of participants. Attempting anything else in the meantime would have been a complete waste of time. Reading through just one volume on those stacks would take more time than had been allotted for the entire project. The best I could hope for was to parse through them enough to determine which volumes and loose documents belonged to which loan participant so I could put them together for shipping. That alone would take all day and probably into the night.

When the secretary finally brought me the list of lenders, she made an off-handed comment as she turned to leave that registered in my mind—and not in a good way.

"This is what Mr. Nathanson's secretary was able to send me. It turns out he won't be back in the office until next Tuesday. But if you have any questions, Blotnick should be able to answer them when he calls, since the borrower is his client in Mexico."

Nathanson was out of his office until next Tuesday? Both unreachable until Blotnick found a moment to call? A project I'd never worked on dumped in my lap without warning or any explanation other than that given by Nathanson's former secretary? At that point, I felt like a soldier crossing a battlefield who suddenly hears a *click* under his foot and realizes he has just triggered a landmine.

Even with the list of participants, I quickly came to the

realization that without more information—like what factors set forth in the loan terms might distinguish which of countless similar-looking documents each lending institution was to receive—the task I'd been given was futile. For each of the more than thirty participants, there were literally hundreds of documents—powers of attorney, proofs of funds, reps and warranties, addendums, exhibits, and the like. And many of these cross-referenced other banks and lending institutions names entitled to docs of their own.

Sitting there in the one small space not buried in stacks of paper, I felt a tear fall down my cheek. Professional? Who cared! This job sucked and was sucking me down a drain with it. Besides, the office door was closed. And even if it wasn't, I was too screwed by this point to care less if anyone saw me crying. Worse, there was absolutely nothing I could do to unscrew myself other than walk out the door and just quit. And I wasn't ready to do that yet.

Just then I heard the door handle turning. I scrambled to wipe the tears off my face as the door started to open. There was probably not a single person in this entire firm who would even care about how I was feeling at that moment, but I at least cared that no one else know it.

As it turned out, the person at the door was Mr. Blotnick's older secretary I'd walked past several weeks earlier when I'd been called to Blotnick's office for his tutorial on the meaning of family. Smiling, she asked politely, "Hi. Am I interrupting?"

Trying to regroup, I quickly wiped the look of frustration—and did I mention the tears?—from my face before responding sheepishly, "No. Come on in. What's up?"

She stepped into the office. I assumed she'd come in to tell me that her boss was now available to talk about the project or some such. But I was wrong. Very wrong.

"Well, let me just say at the beginning that I know I could be fired for this, but I feel you need to hear it anyway. So, may I?"

Expecting something bad, but also thinking the day couldn't get much worse than it already was, I nodded. "Fire away. I'll let you know right out the gate that I'm not in a position to get anyone fired, so you're pretty safe. What's on your mind?"

"Well, here goes. I'm a Christian, and I believe my Lord speaks to me from time to time. Just a few minutes ago as I was walking back to my desk, I'm pretty sure I heard him tell me to come down here to talk with you."

"Your Lord?" was all I could think to ask.

"Yes—my Lord Jesus Christ. I'm sorry. I assumed you would know that. He wants me to let you know that he wants you to know him better."

Wow! Not what I was expecting to hear! "Really? I must say that's—well, different! What does that mean?"

In truth, my first thought was, *In that case, I would think the least he could have done is send Nathanson to help me with all these documents of his!*

Unable to read my thoughts, the secretary continued, "I'm not entirely sure, but I have a friend I think my Lord wants you to meet. Her name is Savannah Georgia Booth. She might have some things to tell you that he wants you to hear. Only if you want to, of course. Anyway, give it some thought and let me know if you do so I can call and make the arrangements. I'm at extension 268."

"Thank you. I'll let you know."

With that, she smiled and left, closing the door behind her.

Well, that's not something you hear every day, I said to myself. As I turned to start the work before me, I thought about how remarkable it was that this woman had been willing to do what she'd just done.

Of course Blotnick's secretary had been with the firm for over twenty years, long enough to recognize just what an untenable situation her boss had placed me in. Maybe she was just a nice enough person to feel empathy for any young associate in such a difficult position. But she'd also been around long enough to know that secretaries had been fired for far less than what she'd just done. My reporting her for religious harassment and unsolicited proselytizing is all it would take. This made it even more amazing, notwithstanding any possible empathy for my situation, that she'd been willing to take that personal risk.

But why bother? What did she have to gain? Nothing that I could tell. That in itself was a large part of why her suggestion that I meet her friend took root, but only weeks later.

For what remained of that day I set any further such thoughts aside to return to the task at hand as best I could. Somewhere around ten that night, I felt reasonably confident I'd arranged all documents in their proper order. After packing them up in boxes, I made arrangements for them to be shipped the following morning to the respective lenders. I'd missed the 5:00 p.m. deadline. But so what if they arrived a day later than Blotnick had wanted! This was the best I could do.

As to reading each document carefully for mistakes or typos, that was an impossibility in the time allowed. So I was happy to leave it there, resting on the assurance that no reasonable person could possibly disagree with me on that point.

I was feeling pretty good as I drove home and had forgotten the offer made by Blotnick's secretary to meet her friend. Maybe the *click* I thought I'd detected earlier that morning wasn't the landmine that would destroy my career after all.

I just had no way of knowing that this project was a bomb that came with a delayed fuse.

Acquire wisdom! Acquire understanding! Do not…. turn away from the words of my mouth.[2]

Then Elisha prayed and said, "O Lord, I pray, open his eyes that he may see." And the Lord opened the servant's eyes and he saw ... the mountain was full of horses and chariots of fire all around Elisha.[1]

~

12

HELP FROM A CRIPPLED ANGEL

About two weeks later, I arrived at the office to hear another message on my answering machine from Blotnick. "Mr. Nichols, please come to my office as soon as you get this message."

Considering the outcome of the last message I'd received from Blotnick, it would be an understatement to say I was less than thrilled. I acknowledged Blotnick's secretary with a smile as I walked past her into his office. I hadn't seen her since she'd dropped by to talk to me, and she gave no indication that conversation had ever occurred as she nodded for me to go on in.

The moment I took a seat opposite Blotnick's desk, he brought up the project from two weeks earlier. I could see he was upset and so I began mentally preparing an explanation of why the boxes hadn't shipped out by his 5:00 p.m. deadline.

But again I was wrong.

"We're getting calls from all the Eurobond participants. Apparently, there are errors in the docs you sent them that Nathanson and his team in New York are attempting to remedy as we speak."

"That can't be," I reassured him. "I double-checked that the correct documents for each participant were in the right box before sealing them and sending them out for pick up."

"That's not the problem," he responded angrily. "They got the right documents. The problem is that there are mistakes in the documents you failed to catch and correct. Erroneous loan amounts and due dates. Errors in their payment schedules. Enough of them that it has embarrassed the firm."

"How was I supposed to know that?" I tried to respond in a useless attempt to defend myself. "I was not given any of that information nor told to double-check the details of each doc. I was just given a list of lending institutions and told to organize and ship the docs appropriate to each. Even if I'd been provided such information, it still would have been impossible, given the time frame I had been given."

Then came the explosion of the landmine I thought I had been spared. To my astonishment, Blotnick said in a voice that could only be described as a controlled scream, "You're an attorney. We aren't paying you to just be a mailing clerk. *Of course* it was your responsibility to double-check the details of each doc before sending them out to the participants. If you didn't have the information necessary to do that, it was your responsibility to get it. I can't even begin to tell you what your screwup means for the firm and for your career."

"But, sir, with all due respect—what about Nathanson? He's the one responsible for the creation of those docs. Why are any mistakes in them my problem and not his? He wasn't even around for me to get the information from him on the single day I had this project. Where was he?"

The instant I asked this question, I knew I was a dead man walking. Plain and simple, Blotnick had chosen me to be the guy to fall on the landmine and absorb the brunt of the explosion so as to protect not only Blotnick's reputation but that of his protégé Nathanson.

I now realized as well that the missing "edge" for which the other partners had passed Nathanson up earlier that year undoubtedly included his lack of attention to such details and his lack of the ethics necessary to assume responsibility for his own mistakes. But neither was a point Blotnick was prepared to concede, much less take a personal hit for. Whether he'd known in advance or had only belatedly learned of Nathanson's errors from the participants, it was clear both Blotnick and Nathanson had agreed I should take the blast Nathanson's sloppy work had set in place months before I'd even become involved.

Suffice it to say, for me the detonation of this belated professional landmine did not feel good. I offered to help Nathanson get the docs back and make the necessary changes. That was when I discovered the blow was going to be fatal.

"That won't be necessary," Blotnick said. "Nathanson will be taking care of that in New York with his team. But the hours you billed the client for this project will be written off. We're not going to give you credit for work you didn't do. If that affects your meeting your quota for required billables, you'll just have to make that up somewhere else later. Thank you. That's all for now."

And with that, I was summarily dismissed.

I could see it unfolding. Blotnick would apologize to the Eurobond participants for the mistakes. Nathanson would correct his errors. Then both would smooth it over with the client while any partners who came to learn of the blunder would be told the errors were mine and mine alone, conveniently failing to mention that the low-level associate on whom blame had been placed could not possibly have known there were any errors to be remedied.

In short, I was the lamb designated to be placed on the firm's sacrificial altar to atone for their sins. Not a fun place for any junior associate to be.

But such is life in the Big Firms where—except on the rare occasion when it can be made to look like guacamole—it is usually true that manure—human or otherwise—does roll downhill.

Leaving Blotnick's office that morning, I paused at his secretary's desk, desperately trying to think of a way to make what had just landed on me roll back uphill to Nathanson. That's when I remembered her offer of two weeks earlier to meet some friend of hers about God. If I ever needed God's help it was now! Meeting this friend was starting to sound like a pretty good idea.

"Why don't you call your friend you told me about," I

suggested as casually as I could muster, "If she's around, I think this looks like a good day to talk with her."

"Will do," the secretary replied quietly. "If you stick by the phone in your office, I'll let you know in a few minutes if she can do it today."

So it was that I found myself later that day climbing a long, dark stairway to the apartment of a lady named Savannah Georgia Booth. At least it seemed dark and the climb long, though perhaps it was only my mood since her apartment was on the second floor. I had left the office "early" again to make the trip, but this time around I didn't give a lump of brown steaming pudding what either Blotnick or the firm might think about it. Nuts to both them and their billable hours.

The woman who responded to my knock on the door was somewhere in her late sixties with salt and pepper hair, seated in a wheelchair. I found her kindly expression reassuring and my nervousness over this encounter began abating.

"Come in. I've been expecting you," she said with a smile. After backing her wheelchair up, she gestured for me to take a seat on her sofa. As I did so, she wheeled across the room to pick up a Bible, then returned to position herself directly in front of me, her Bible resting on her lap.

"You can see that I'm crippled," she began, her gaze radiating warmth. "So let me start by telling you how that came to be."

Then she unhurriedly recounted how she had been in an automobile accident many years ago. She and her daughter were traveling down a rainy stretch of highway on their way home from a prayer meeting when her car hit an oil slick. The car rolled several times before hitting a guardrail that ran along the edge of the road. She'd been thrown from the car against the guardrail, breaking her back. All she knew then was that she couldn't move her legs. She had no way of knowing that she'd be a paraplegic bound to a wheelchair for the rest of her life.

Her last conscious memory of the event was looking over at her daughter, who'd been left pinned underneath the overturned roof with the weight of the car resting on her lower abdomen. Ms. Booth could hear her daughter pleading for help but couldn't move to help her. In the midst of her own pain, all she could do was plead to God to save her daughter.

Then mercifully she passed out. But her memory didn't end there. She found herself floating above the crash site, looking down not only at her daughter, who had stopped moving, but also at her own body, lying unconscious in the mud. At first she believed she had died. Then she heard a voice she knew to be the voice of her Lord, assuring her that all she was viewing was to the good. Her daughter was now with him. She, Savannah Georgia Booth, would be spared but left a cripple as an example to let others who were broken—like me, I presumed—and living in a broken world—again, I supposed, like mine had been by Blotnick earlier that day—know of his love.

For the next two hours, we sat in her living room while she talked to me about God's purpose and plan for his children. She was fascinating, and her stories were compelling. But about 3:00 p.m., I was starting to get nervous. My

Mega-Firm conditioning was such that I felt guilty about my absence from the office and was worried I'd be missed. Accused, in fact, for shirking my duties to my *adopted* family.

But when I stood to explain my need to get back to work, she said with a gentle firmness, "Sit back down. Please. The Lord is not done. There is more he needs you to know this day before you leave."

Though gently conveyed, it was not a request, and I felt I had no other choice than to re-take my seat. For the next three hours, she continued her narrative, rapidly rifling from one passage to another in the Bible on her lap to validate each point she was making.

The short story of it all was that she explained Jesus's love for me. That his love was so great he had given his life for me so that I might be saved from death and have the gift of eternal life.

That in time I would come to both trust him and love him.

That in time I would come to want to give my life to serve his Kingdom's purposes here on earth in return.

That I would grow to look to him for his companionship and guidance as I traveled on my journey through life.

That I would come to depend upon him for my protection and victory in the future battles I would face in life.

That I would come to realize that those battles and other adversities I experienced were really only part of a much larger war being fought in a spiritual realm.

That God needs broken people like her *and me* to help the forces of God overcome the evil that seeks to control and bedevil what is nothing less than a world that is broken.

Truthfully, of all the verses she used that day to make these points, the only one that stuck with me was from the sixth chapter of Ephesians.

> *Finally, be strong in the Lord and*
> *in the strength of His might. Put on*
> *the full armor of God, so that you will*
> *be able to stand firm against*
> *the schemes of the devil. For our*
> *struggle is not against flesh and blood,*
> *but against the powers, against the*
> *world forces of this darkness, against*
> *the spiritual forces of wickedness in*
> *the heavenly places.*[2]

I'm guessing that was because it reminded me of Blotnick.

Eventually, she finished, but when I least wanted her to. In those few hours, she had conveyed to me more than I had ever been able to put together in a cohesive form from all the evenings spent with my Papa and all the church services I had attended in my youth with my parents. I was exhausted, but also left feeling both excited and somehow mysteriously at peace.

By the time we said our goodbyes, it was nearly six o'clock. She thanked me for coming. I in turn should have thanked God more than I did for allowing me to spend those few hours with Savannah Georgia Booth. Given the traffic at that hour, going back downtown to the office was not worth the effort. So I headed home instead with a certain excitement to reflect upon all I had learned.

Later that year, Nathanson made it to the top of the pyramid. Blotnick had succeeded in getting him the "edge" he needed to be made a partner. Not long afterward, Blotnick suffered a massive stroke from which he never recovered. Whether the two events were related by way of cause and effect, I may never know. But I wouldn't be surprised.

What I did know was that for me the Mega-Firm pyramid I had been trying to climb was no longer one I wanted to scale. Following my visit with Ms. Booth, my priorities began to shift. I soon came to the decision that there had to be more to life than striving to obtain the carrot the firm kept dangling in front of my nose.

Eventually, I moved on. After all, I came to realize, how much worse could a solo practice be? Even so, I am amazed that I have remained on the Mega-Firm's alumni roster now for nearly thirty-five years, receiving their invites to occasional events. Each invite lets me know how much they value their alums. I in turn have studiously avoided them all in case they might be serving something like bad guacamole.

Over the years since leaving the Mega-Firm, I've often thought of Savannah Georgia Booth and her friend, Mr. Blotnick's faithful secretary. I never saw either of them again after that afternoon in Ms. Booth's apartment. In fact, they both seemed to have just mysteriously appeared and then disappeared from my life.

Which isn't to say that their impact upon my life didn't

last a lifetime. It has. Were these two ladies angels sent to redirect the priorities and direction of my life? Who knows? The only thing I do know for sure is that I expect to see them both again at some point in the future. When I do, I'm confident that Savannah Georgia Booth will happily no longer be seated in a wheelchair. And if indeed it turns out she was an angel? So much the better. How cool would that be?

Either way, I can't wait to let her know about some of the things that happened in my life after our visit.

～

Then the devil left him, and behold, angels came and began to minister to him.[3]

Even when the fool walks along the road, his sense is lacking and he demonstrates to everyone that he is a fool. [1]

∽

13

HOOKING UP WITH MR. MURDER

It wasn't long after my encounters with Ms. Booth and the Nathanson landmine that I left the Mega-Firm. Was the decision mine or the firm's?

I would have to say both.

I wasn't thrilled with the idea of experiencing another Mega-Firm, so I changed course and used what little money my wife and I had been able to save to open an office of my own in a small community about thirty miles from my folks' ranch. Near enough to Los Angeles to suit me, while also near enough to the "country life" that I hoped would suit my wife.

In the beginning, it most certainly didn't pay what I was sure I was worth. On a bright note, it gave me more time to do things like be with my family, return to church, and eventually attend a weekly Bible study with some of the men I met along the way.

I wasn't sure about what field of law I should specialize in, but in short order found myself *specializing* in just about anything that would bring in enough money to cover the office overhead and put food on the table. There were some months in that first year that if I could have made an extra buck or two selling whiskey out of my car trunk like Papa, I have to confess I would have.

Then I learned that a lawyer both willing and available at the drop of a hat could get occasional criminal cases involving indigent clients assigned to them at the nearby municipal courthouse. The court clerks handed these cases out to their favored members of the local bar. So keeping the lesson of the guacamole rolling uphill in mind, I went out of my way to be very nice indeed to these clerks at every opportunity. It wasn't long before I had a reasonably good criminal defense practice. Even if most of my clients were broke, at least the clerks were staying fat and sassy from all the donuts I dropped off on their desk two or three mornings a week.

The indigent clients I undertook to defend had a constitutional right to an attorney just like everybody else. But because they were too poor to afford one, the county had to find them one—like me—and pay a modest fee. The remuneration wasn't much, and a low-rung criminal defense practice was a long way from doing Eurobond transactions on the twenty-second floor of a downtown high rise. But it paid the rent on my ground-level office and wasn't nearly as dull.

That is the short story of how I moved into the legal arena of criminal defense law and so ultimately came to meet characters like P. Cummings, D. Hewitt, and Brock M.

Cummings was an attorney who was a legend—at least in his own mind. He particularly liked being known around the local legal community as Mr. Capital Murder. And in one sense it was true. He had handled more of such cases than almost any other attorney around.

This wasn't because he was particularly great at it. As I eventually came to learn, he wasn't! That is, not better than a lot of other attorneys roaming the court hallways. He got appointed to so many cases mainly because he was a long-standing member of the Elks Lodge. Not long after joining, he became a favored drinking buddy of another Lodge member named D. Hewitt, who just happened to be the local municipal court judge and whose duties included the appointment of those cases. Whether or not he was sober when he did it was a separate issue. If Cummings and Hewitt had any strong suit for which both were legitimately legendary, it was their ability to drink.

Cumming's beverage of choice was Johnny Walker Red Label Talls. And Hewitt's? From what I could see over the years I knew him, any drink placed within arm's length. Both could put five or six away at lunch and still make it back to court to finish any business remaining on their calendars for that day. How well they did for the defendants and other members of the public that happened to come across their paths was a matter of opinion. How many drinks they downed to forget it all after finishing with those clients was anybody's guess.

That daily routine could explain why death penalty cases didn't faze Cummings. The Talls probably helped numb him to things like having at least three clients sitting on death row. Or at least that was the most he admitted to when I met him.

Being unaware of the aforementioned other than his moniker of Mr. Capital Murder, I considered my first association with Cummings to be somewhat of an honor. This happened when Judge Hewitt's clerk called us both in one day to represent a pair of male co-defendants who'd been jointly charged in the same criminal complaint, along with a third defendant who was female.

I was the first to arrive to Judge Hewitt's courtroom that particular day. When Cummings came in, I was a bit shocked—read, *kind of excited*—to learn I'd been placed on a case with such a local luminary. I understood why Hewitt's clerk would call Cummings but had to assume the clerk was throwing me a bone because of my persistent courting of her services via the diligent application of my donut theory.

While we waited for Hewitt's clerk to arrive back from lunch to give us the necessary paperwork, Cummings and I started chatting. As a relative newbie, I found this a bit intimidating.

Cummings was easily ten years my senior. Because of the two-and-a-half-inch heels on his trademark cowboy boots, he stood several inches taller than my own six-foot frame. His flared pants were consistently worn at least one size too tight, a prominent enough feature of his persona that not even a casual observer could overlook at a hundred paces. It made me wonder if the reason one attorney in the courthouse always referred to Cummings as

"*Mr. Horse Balls*" wasn't necessarily the tribute to his bold courtroom demeanor I had always before presumed.

All to say, I was feeling a bit overshadowed in more ways than one. Desperate to divert any attention away from me, I quickly steered our conversation around to the death penalty part of his practice. "So I hear you've done a lot of capital murder cases."

"Yep," he replied.

"I've never done one. Why do you take on such complicated and time-consuming cases? Aren't they a lot of work?"

Before responding, Cummings gave me his award-winning smile coupled with a dramatic pause. As I got to know him later, I came to admire the maneuver. For one thing, it drew attention away from his watery, booze-soaked eyes while allowing him to use the pause and those same watery eyes to carefully appraise the person he happened to be talking to—in this case, me.

Then he responded with a bravado I later came to learn was another hallmark of his personality. "I do them, Kiddo, because I'm the only son-of-a-gun around here who has the cojones to do them."

I couldn't deny this to be at least partly true, given the conspicuous evidence he was presenting me—and, for that matter, anyone within ten paces of those skin-tight flared pants.

But it was also probably true that most attorneys are afraid of the work and responsibility that comes with such cases. A contributing factor is that capital murder cases typically go to trial—especially if the district attorney is inclined to settle for nothing less than the death penalty. And when such cases are lost at trial, the verdict is guaranteed to be appealed. What this means for the defense attorney is that the trial transcripts will be scrutinized numerous times by numerous people looking for any reason to overturn the verdict. Which oft-times is most easily achieved if they can successfully accuse the defense attorney of incompetence. So for most attorneys, it becomes work for which only the bold will apply.

Evidently Cummings didn't seem to have any worries about the impact on his own professional career. He went on to tell me, "I discovered early on that it was okay to jump into that pond—it's neither too deep nor too cold. In fact, Kiddo, you might try one of those cases yourself some time. Just jump in. You'll find out pretty quickly the water is just fine. You won't drown, and you might just find you'll learn a helluva lot."

He paused again before adding with a wink, "Besides that, Kiddo, they are the only court-appointed cases where the county is willing to pay you just about whatever you want to bill them. Sometimes over a hundred grand—and mind you, that's just for one case."

Back then that was a lot of money, so I asked, "How do you get appointed to those cases? I've heard they aren't just handed out to any attorney out there."

"Officially, Kiddo, you have to be on the death penalty panel. But really it's all about politics, son. Politics. Just take it easy, and I'll teach you the ropes soon enough. Just be patient, and let's see how we do on the case we're getting today. What do we have for today? That's the question, huh, Kiddo?"

"Yeah, I suppose it is," I agreed.

"Then what are you waiting for? There's the clerk coming in right now. Let's get to it and pick up the paperwork."

Getting there first, Cummings reached out to take both packets the clerk had laid out for us on the rail beside her desk. Each contained the arrest reports and charges being brought against one of our new clients. I didn't realize at first that Cummings had grabbed both. When I asked the clerk for my paperwork, she threw Cummings a cynical glance that told me he had both. Not wanting to seem pushy, I deferred to his expertise and waited for him to give me mine whenever he was ready.

He rifled through the docs, then eventually handed me a packet. I'd assumed—again based on his expertise and experience—that he'd be taking the client with the more serious charges and was just checking to make sure he got the right one.

I was wrong.

As it turned out, which client I was to represent had apparently been decided by Cummings' slight-of-hand. By reviewing both packets, he'd determined that I would have the privilege of representing the really bad guy while his own client would be the lesser-involved accomplice. The third defendant was a female named Loretta. But she didn't concern us as the clerk let us know she was being represented by privately retained counsel.

In short, my guy was facing over a hundred years in

state prison for, among other things, the sexual molestation of a minor. Whereas Cummings' client was looking at a maximum of ten years for some drug-related charges he had in common with my client.

This mattered because the client I was being handed would take a lot more research time than his accomplice due to the legal complexities, and I was already aware that Judge Hewitt didn't pay attorneys for such work.

Shortly after I'd started doing cases in his court, he'd called me into his chambers to admonish me about my bill for a client he had given me to defend. Specifically, he was concerned about the three hours for research I'd had the audacity to charge the county for.

"The county doesn't pay attorneys to do legal research," he informed me. "We want attorneys who know what they're doing. That means attorneys who know the law and don't have to go looking it up. Any research you feel you need to do, do it on your own dime."

In short, Judge Hewitt couldn't care less whether such research was necessary to help a client or would have an impact on the outcome of a case. He didn't mind if it happened. He just didn't want to hear about it—especially on any bill to the county he might have to approve.

But for any defense counsel with professional integrity, that didn't mean such research didn't still need to be done. This realization was hitting me with both barrels as I shuffled through the documents I'd just been handed, barely taking in Cummings' continued commentary.

"Well, Kiddo, if I were you, I'd start by getting an investigator appointed. Then start him looking for alibi witnesses and any other sort of stuff you and he might find helpful. District attorneys around here take child molestation charges pretty seriously, so your guy is gonna be looking at you to stand in the gap between him and a pretty bleak future."

Still thinking Cummings must have made a mistake, I started to plead, "Now, wait a minute! Shouldn't you take the bad guy? I mean, you know what you're doing here. I don't."

He flashed me his award-winning smile. "Nonsense, Kiddo. You need the experience, not me. But I'll tell you what. Once you've read the report, talk to me, and I'll let you know if I can think of anything helpful to get you started."

He then chuckled. "I just hope your fingers are limber, Kiddo."

"Why?"

"Because you're going to be typing a helluva lot of motions before this case is over."

"Like what? What kind of motions are you thinking about?"

"I don't know, Kiddo. That's your job. You're going to have to hit the books and look for any loopholes in the law you can find. Anyway, keep me posted on your progress, Kiddo," he tossed over his shoulder as he started to leave the court to meet his new client.

But before he could disappear, I called out, "Hey, Cummings! Really, don't you think it would be better if we swapped defendants? After all, you have a lot more experience so you won't have to do all the research this is going to require. It doesn't make sense for me to take the heavyweight."

"Give me a break, Kiddo!" Cummings snorted. "I'm doing you a favor. Just think of all the experience you're going to get before this is all over."

And though I didn't know it at the time, he was right. Eventually when I could look back on it all, I would come to appreciate how much his little manipulation contributed to my becoming a much better lawyer. For that I appreciate P. Cummings immensely to this very day.

Back then, however, those were not my thoughts as I watched him walk off to interview his client. I was left with no other choice than to do the same. My head still spinning, I headed down the hallway toward the interview rooms. So much for getting paid for a lot of the work this was going to require! At least until I could get the case out of Hewitt's municipal court and up to the superior court with a different judge who would hopefully not disparage the research an attorney was duty-bound to do. Mentally, I resolved to make this happen as quickly as possible, then I hurried to meet my new client.

The hallway that led to the interview rooms ran the full length of the building with doors to several courtrooms on one side. On the other side was the door to the prisoner lockup room and adjacent attorney interview cubicles. I was always impressed by the stark contrast between the wood-paneled courtrooms with their leather-bound chairs, sophisticated lighting, and generally distinguished appearance and this bleak, ugly passageway beyond which society's fallen were held in custody while awaiting their day in court.

I called out my client's name to the bailiff in charge of lockup, then searched out an empty interview room. After closing the metal door behind me, I took a seat at a metal desk on a cold metal stool solidly anchored into the concrete floor. The only other item in the room was a wall phone by which I could communicate to the phone on the other side of a bulletproof Plexiglas window separating the attorney from the inmate's side of the cubicle, which was a mirror image of mine.

I could hear a deputy calling my client's name into the general lockup holding tank as I started rifling through the sheriff's report attached to my client's formal criminal complaint. I quickly learned that Brock M. was not even remotely one of society's good guys. In fact, he was really a pretty good bad guy judging by his county résumé—that is, the county's paperwork detailing all his prior offenses.

He'd been in state prison at least twice and had visited the county's "Graybar Hotel," as the main jail facility in downtown Los Angeles was commonly termed, more times than I wanted to count for a variety of criminal behavior. And all this by the age of twenty-eight.

In sum, Brock's life seemed to be a case study of bad decisions that led to bad behavior that led to multiple arrests for multiple reasons. Apparently, he had not bene-fitted along the way from the education others might have gained from such experiences that just might have led him to try to do something different—i.e., legal—the next time around. In short, *being bad* was a career path he'd settled upon and grown comfortable with long before I met him.

Which was a shame because if you set all that aside, Brock really did seem like a nice guy on that first encounter. Once he'd finally arrived, we both picked up the phones on our respective sides of the Plexiglas separating us, and I quickly found he was easy to talk to. I couldn't help noticing that he was both tall and strong. But he also came across as non-threatening and a guy who could appreciate a good joke when one popped up in the course of our conversation.

He certainly didn't seem the kind of guy who would sexually assault the four-year-old daughter of his meth-queen girlfriend as the district attorney was alleging. Oh, and did I mention the fact that he passionately maintained his innocence throughout the following months leading up to his trial?

"After all, I have standards," he calmly told me that first day and every day we met after that. "I would never do anything close to what they're claiming. Truth is, if I ever came across anyone doing any of the stuff they're accusing me of, I'd probably kill them."

Perhaps he thought I would find that comforting and persuasive. In a strange way, I guess you could say I did, at least for a while.

Was he endearing?

No, not exactly.

Did he leave me feeling there was a spark of something in him worthy of being redeemed?

Maybe just a little at first.

Did his argument contain a kernel of twisted logic?

Yes, because anyone who did what they were accusing him of probably should be shot.

At the end of the day, what bothered me most about his case was how one was to ever know the actual truth. After all, the charges were based on the word of his former girlfriend Loretta, the third defendant in this case, who not only wasn't the best mother in the world but hated Brock with a passion. In short, she was not exactly an unbiased witness.

All I knew was that my duty to Brock involved compelling the People of the State—i.e., the district attorney—to prove their case against my client beyond a reasonable doubt. With his unwavering professions of innocence, I was certainly motivated to do the best I could on his behalf.

It took eleven months to complete pre-trial preparation —months packed with a host of various legalities to prepare our defense. In a word, Cummings had been correct. My typing of motions consumed a lot of my time during those months. Witness interviews. Investigator reports. Lab tests. Medical and psychiatric exams. All resulting in what seemed like a mountain of various motions that in turn required numerous hearings and continuances to allow the court to hear arguments and issue its rulings.

Then, by contrast, there was Cummings' contributions to the case. Andy Warhol is reputed to have once said something like, "Ninety percent of success can be attributed to a person's willingness to just show up."

Whether or not Warhol was correct, I learned in the course of the pre-trial phase of the case that P. Cummings and Andy had much in common on this point at least.

The filing of the complaint was such that Cumming's client and mine along with the mother of the little girl, a co-defendant on charges of child abuse and narcotics possession, would all be tried together. Which meant that Cummings benefitted from many of the motions I filed. He would just show up at the last minute before hearings on any given motion. Then if he considered it beneficial, he'd simply tell the court he'd be joining in on my motion for his own client.

Just before the hearing, he'd draw me to the side and say something like, "Hey Kiddo, give me the Reader's Digest version. Why are we here today? Quick before the judge takes the bench!"

It didn't take me long to realize he hadn't even bothered to read any of the related documents I'd sent his office at the same time they were filed with the court. I'd give him the short story he asked for, but it didn't often help me, as between the two of us I was always the guy who seemed to have to do the heavy lifting. He'd let me present the argument to the judge while he smiled and nodded, conveying the impression that what I was saying had great merit and also applied to his client.

Conversely, whenever it started to appear to Cummings that the judge was probably going to deny my motion, he'd give the court a look to distance himself as if to suggest to anyone who might be interested—like the judge—that he had no idea why I had brought the particular motion.

To his credit, whichever way it turned out he was always there to either encourage me or soften the blow. Regardless of how the judge ruled, he'd turn that award-winning smile on me and say something like, "Keep up the good work, Kiddo. You're doing great."

It was just what I needed to keep me moving down the road toward trial. What never occurred to me until later was that maybe God knew this too and was using Cummings to accomplish that purpose. At the time, all it left me thinking as I watched him leave the court was, *Thanks, Cummings. I couldn't have done it without you!*

Either way, it was clear Cummings was only too happy to take a free ride on my work, which he did all the way down the pike right up to the day of jury selection. But finally the day of reckoning arrived. The date for trial was set. Cummings wouldn't be able to avoid working anymore. The trial was something even he couldn't avoid.

Or so I thought!

~

Dead flies make a perfumer's oil stink, so a little foolishness is weightier than wisdom and honor.[2]

Strong drink is bitter to those who drink it.[1]

≈

14

BETTER LATE THAN NEVER, BUT BETTER NEVER LATE

Due to an overburdened calendar, the local superior court where most of my motions had been heard was not available for the actual trial. This left us having to schlep to the only court with an opening in its calendar, nearly sixty miles away.

To me, the drive back and forth would be pretty much a waste of time. To Cummings, it meant we could carpool so he could play catch-up on what he'd missed by picking my brain along the way. A brilliant maneuver on his part as it allowed him to get ready for the trial with as little effort as possible. This included reading all the docs in my trial brief and asking an endless number of questions about the facts my investigator and I had uncovered over the past months while I chauffeured him to and from the trial court.

He'd also decided from the start that this meant taking my car, using my gas, and having me to pick up the daily parking fee. Not to mention the lunch tab. According to Cummings, this was so all food and transportation expenses could appear on just one bill to the county— mine. In truth, I came to realize, Cummings was just cheap. Bottom line, he didn't want to pay for anything if he could avoid it.

Every morning as we'd arrive at the courthouse, a couple reporters who had been following the case from the beginning would try to get our statements. Politely but firmly, we'd either ignore them or tell them we had nothing to say based on Cummings's philosophy: "Never give the press anything too soon. It can come back and bite you in the ass later, Kiddo. Trust me. We'll know when the time is right to talk with them. Timing is everything, Kiddo."

The jury selection process alone continued for several days. During this time, Cummings established another routine—having me drive us to the same restaurant for lunch every day, which happened to be quite a distance from the courthouse.

Why there? The bar in the back still permitted smoking and drinking during lunch. Unfortunately, the early morning commute, trial, and general routine of having to be present on a timely and consistent basis had begun wearing on Cummings. One indication of this erosion was how much more he was drinking each day at lunch than the day before.

By the fourth day when he ordered his *sixth* Johnnie Walker Red Label Tall, suffice it to say I was more than mildly bothered. I wasn't drinking and considered that a trial was no time for him to be doing so either. At least not until after it was over. Cummings was apparently not too terribly burdened with such concerns nor with the concept of needing to be prompt.

One day, we were already fifteen minutes past the time we were to have resumed our *voir dire*—i.e., the questioning of prospective jurors to determine which ones we wanted on the final jury. This didn't even include the twenty-minute drive back to the courthouse. When I pointed this out, Cummings just shrugged.

"Don't worry, Kiddo. You won't miss anything. Haven't you learned by now that a lawyer's job operates on the principle of hurry up and wait? Well, I long ago shifted my *modus operandi*. Now I don't hurry up so much. That way I don't have to wait for those judges who are always telling lawyers to hurry up, then take their own sweet time to show up themselves. Make sense, Kiddo? So calm down. It's all going to be just fine."

I chose to ignore the infinitesimally small kernel of logic his statement contained and urged, "Cummings, you may be right, but I don't think so this time. The judge seemed pretty serious about finishing jury selection today. So forget that drink and let's go."

With pointed slowness, Cummings set down his unfinished drink. A smirk of agitation instead of his trademark smile revealed his annoyance over leaving a glass still filled with his favorite adult beverage. "Fine, let's go then. Get the bill, will ya?"

As I paid the tab that included his six Red Label Talls, I

wondered whether the judge approving the lunch receipts would just assume that three of them were mine.

Probably.

That's just swell! I told myself sourly. But I soon got over my own annoyance in the relief that he'd agreed to leave and we were finally heading back to court.

Upon our return to courthouse, as Cummings and I walked down the long hallway toward the assigned court-room, I immediately spotted a problem. Nobody was waiting outside the courtroom for the bailiff to unlock the courtroom door and let them in. In fact, the hall was completely empty.

That could only mean one thing. Cummings's hurry up and wait theory wasn't in operation. Instead, everybody, including the entire jury pool, had been on time and was already inside the courtroom. That is, everybody except Cummings and me.

When Cummings and I entered through the double doors leading into the court, the room was silent enough to hear a pin drop. But not for lack of people. Bailiff, clerk, court reporter, and district attorney were all in their rightful places. Selected jurors were in the jury box. The remaining jury pool was seated in the audience section.

All were looking silently back and forth from us to the judge as though watching an episode of their favorite reality television show. From his place on the bench, the judge slowly swiveled his icy glare from the two of us to the clock on the wall.

I had never before appreciated how painfully audible

the steps of two men walking down a linoleum-tiled aisle could be. The embarrassment of all those eyeballs laser-focused upon the two of us made me want to stop in my tracks. At least it had that effect on me. I doubt Cummings in his pickled state could have possibly appreciated fully the chilled atmosphere, much less care as much about it as I did. But until I arrived at where I should have been almost an hour before, stopping was not an option.

When we finally got to our table, the judge said nothing at first, his silence deafening as he slowly turned his head to look one last time at the clock on the wall. With continued slowness, he lowered his gaze to the jury.

"Ladies and gentlemen, I apologize for this delay. Typically, attorneys are not so inconsiderate as to return forty minutes late from a one-hour lunch. Perhaps there is a reason lunch was extended to become a one-hour-and-forty-minute experience. Though I seriously doubt it would be a legitimate reason any of us would find acceptable. So let me first thank each of you for being prompt, returning on time, and secondly, I thank you all for your patience."

He again went silent. Very slowly, he turned toward Cummings and me before breaking the silence. "Gentlemen, thank you for joining us."

A long pause.

"In the future, let us understand something."

Another long pause.

"For courtesy to be mutually extended to all concerned, breaks for one hour shall henceforth mean *exactly* that— one hour. Is that understood?"

"Your Honor, we do apologize. Please understand that —" I started to offer some lame excuse I could only hope might salvage the situation.

But the judge mercifully interrupted me with a wave of his hand. Like a parent speaking to a wayward infant, he continued: "Counselor, what we all understand is that this mistake shall *not* be repeated, no matter what your excuse may be on this particular day. Should you wish to say something in an attempt to make us understand why we have all been made to sit here awaiting your return for the good part of an hour, I would only admonish you to consider carefully whether we are likely to find what you have to offer even remotely entertaining, much less anything that will improve your present situation."

"Understood, Your Honor. Nothing further, Your Honor," I mumbled. "It won't happen again."

"Very well, then. I think that is the exact assurance we are seeking. Please take a seat and let's get started, shall we?"

As we took our seats, I glanced over at Cummings. He had said nothing, nor did he even try. He was just giving the jury a smile and slight nod of his head as though intending to convey some message. Was he trying to convince them it wasn't his fault we were late? Or that he wasn't as soused as he appeared to me to be? Who could know precisely what Cummings hoped to accomplish. I just hoped they couldn't smell the alcohol on his breath from across the room, because sitting next to him I sure could!

Needless to say, because of this experience our sixty-mile trip back home would have been pretty silent even if Cummings hadn't slept through most of it. When I dropped him off at his house, I did make the point that I didn't want to be late getting to court the next morning. Before we left, the judge had let us know that opening statements were set to start at 9:00 a.m. sharp. To me, that meant at 9:00 a.m. sharp.

"Got it, Kiddo," was all Cummings said before heading toward his front door—or perhaps it would be more accurate to say *wobbled*.

In an abundance of caution, we pulled up to the courthouse an hour early the next morning. It wasn't open, so with nothing better to do, Cummings and I found a seat in the courtyard off to the side of the building. My mind was spinning with all the evidence and testimony based on eleven months of tedious and painstaking preparation I had done for this moment. By Cummings's decree, I would be giving the opening statement for both of our clients so had the responsibility of setting the stage that would hopefully enable the jury to eventually reach a not guilty verdict.

In the distance, I could see the district attorney talking in the courtyard with one of the sheriff deputies involved in the case. Soon another officer joined them, and the three continued the conversation with what seemed to be some degree of animation. I asked Cummings what he thought it was all about.

"I don't know, Kiddo," he teased me with a chuckle. "Probably just putting the finishing touches on their plans for our crucifixion."

I assumed he meant that, given Loretta's anticipated testimony, we were going to get creamed in the trial. "Thanks, Cummings. That's encouraging."

Eventually, the court opened. Cummings and I took our seats. The district attorney and the detective who had worked the case took theirs at a table opposite ours. Then the judge entered. But before the clients could be brought in, the district attorney stood to address the court.

The judge looked annoyed but gestured for the district attorney to say what was on his mind. To my surprise and interest, the district attorney asked for a postponement to discuss what he said were some critical matters with one of his witnesses. The court granted his request, and we all adjourned to the hall. The delay was short, and the bailiff soon came out to let us know we could return to the courtroom.

We again waited for the judge to take his seat. The room was filled with faint murmurings until a door in the rear of the court opened. The ensuing silence was soon broken by a rattling of chains that were attached to our clients' ankles as they were led forward to take their respective seats beside Cummings and me.

What made no sound was the electrocution vest under the ill-fitting shirt and sports coat each client was wearing pursuant to one of the motions I had brought at the very beginning of the pre-trial proceedings. Several days earlier, before the jury pool had been brought in, our clients had arrived with chains securing not only their ankles but also their wrists, which in turn were chained to other chains wrapped around their waists for the entire world to see.

Such security procedures were considered appropriate for high-risk defendants charged with things like murder or child molestation and looking at decades or a lifetime in prison. Otherwise the bailiffs and other sheriff deputies involved might find themselves having to deal with a defendant who could be highly motivated to want to escape from their custody.

But no defendant looks very good with waist chains and handcuffs even when dressed up in a suit. The problem this presents from the defendant's point of view is that the jurors might be persuaded simply by seeing all these additional accoutrements that the defendant must be guilty of something serious. To avoid such a contamination of the jury pool's legally mandated presumption of my client's innocence, I had filed a motion to have any chains visible to potential jurors removed for the duration of the trial. Needless to say, Cummings had immediately joined my motion on behalf of his client.

Of course, the law enforcement present immediately joined the district attorney to oppose my motion. But after what I'd like to think were my compelling arguments about my client's constitutional rights to a fair trial, the judge ruled in my favor, and all chains visible above the waist were replaced by electronic vests while the clients were in the courtroom.

Quite simply, the vest was a restraining device similar in appearance to a bulletproof vest and worn underneath the client's shirt. If either defendant made an unauthorized move or tried to escape, the bailiff could send an electric shock through their bodies that would drop them to the floor like a bag of rocks.

At the time, I had good reason to wonder if that might happen.

But now, behold, I am freeing you today from the chains which are on your hands.[2]

If you have been foolish in exalting yourself ... put your hand on your mouth.[1]

∾

15

PERHAPS SHAKESPEARE SAID IT BEST

On the first morning of trial, the clink of metal under the table was a reminder of the brilliance of my motion. While our clients were still hobbled at the ankles, at least the jury couldn't see their chains as long as their legs remained under the table.

I didn't fully consider the downside of this arrangement until the morning the jury was to take their seats to hear opening arguments. That was when it occurred to me how little I liked my client's arms being unchained. What if he didn't appreciate my defense of him as the trial proceeded? He could grab a pen or pencil on the desk and do me some serious harm before the bailiff could push the "electrocution" button.

Oh, well. Such was a risk I'd just have to assume. What I didn't know yet was that pretty soon it really wouldn't matter.

"All rise!" from the bailiff let us all know it was time to get this show on the road. Once we were on our feet, the judge entered, took his seat, then instructed the bailiff to bring in the jury. But before the bailiff could respond, the district attorney stood up.

"Your Honor, before you bring in the jury, I request to be heard."

The judge looked at him with no small hint of annoyance on his face. "What is it, counselor? I thought we'd dealt with all pre-trial matters. What do you have?"

"I need a few moments with a witness, Your Honor. Could we delay calling in the jury? It will be brief, I assure you."

We were adjourned for a brief break, then called to return to our seats. What came next surprised even the judge.

"Your Honor, the People move to dismiss all charges against both defendants."

I almost broke my neck jerking my head around toward the district attorney in shock.

"Did I just hear you correctly?" the judge demanded.

But before the district attorney could answer, my client burst into an expletive-laced speech, addressing both the district attorney and the detective next to him first, but then extended to just about everybody in the room. "What the %#&!!!! You kept me in lockup for almost a year! Now you just want to dismiss the case and pretend you haven't made my life a living hell for the last eleven months?"

Thinking this was a somewhat inopportune time for my client to be venting, I leaned over to whisper with a patina of urgency in my voice, "Put a lid on it, Brock! This is a good thing for you. What are you trying to do? Get them to change their minds? Are you an idiot? Just keep your mouth shut and don't blow this! Just hold it in for now, and we can talk about this later back in lockup."

He didn't exactly shut up, but at least he notched his angry monologue down to a grumble that only Cummings and I could hear. In the meantime, the district attorney had reassured the judge that he really wanted the case dismissed. Thankfully for us, the judge granted the motion and ordered the bailiffs to return our clients to the central jail holding facility to be processed for release.

With that, two bailiffs accompanied my client as he clinked his way out of the courtroom. My thought was to follow him back to lockup to calm him down and explain further the significance of what had just happened. In short, I wanted to clarify that a dismissal was as good as he could have ever hoped for. That the dark cloud of a possible hundred-year sentence to a state prison hanging over his head for the last year was gone and gone for good. For anybody in Brock's position, it just didn't get any better than that.

To me, this dismissal of all charges seemed like something he should have been happy about. But I was wrong. In fact, when all was said and done, perhaps you could say I was really wrong—in more ways than one.

But we'll take that up later.

It was not until after my conversation with my client that I caught up with Cummings in the hallway to ask him, "What was that about? Why do you think the district attorney did that?"

"Who knows, Kiddo! They never tell you. It may have

had something to do with all the information you acquired and the witnesses you had ready to testify on our side. Or it could have to do with one or more of their witnesses getting cold feet and crumbling. Who knows, and really, Kiddo, who cares! I told you it would all work out, didn't I?"

After the conversation I'd just had with my client, I wasn't so confident he was correct. But one thing I did know was that I didn't want to discuss it with Cummings. For one thing, I wasn't sure he'd care. But it was also in part because as we left the courtroom, a reporter approached to ask the same questions I had just asked Cummings.

Seeing the reporter head our direction, Cummings turned to me, winked, and with his trademark grin said, "Now's the time, Kiddo."

"Time for what?"

The look he gave me suggested I was an idiot. "Now is the time to talk with the press. What else do you think I'm talking about?"

I guessed he thought this should be my moment to shine. All the long months of work and preparation could now pay off. The problem was, I really didn't feel like it. My client was upset. And for different reasons than my client, so was I.

The end result was that I found myself trying to answer the reporter's questions by rambling on in long verbal strings about random legal issues I thought might matter and, I must confess, I sincerely hoped would make me sound brilliant. All the while, Cummings just sat back and took it all in with a smile. That is, until I could think of no more to say and came to a close.

The reporter then turned to Cummings. "Do you have anything to add?"

Cummings's response was the essence of brilliant simplicity. "The case was dismissed because, after all was said and done, it was Shakespearian—much ado about nothing."

With that, he gave the reporter his patented grin, thanked him, and then said to me in a voice calculated to be loud enough for the reporter to hear, "Come on, Kiddo, we gotta get on the road and head back. I've got other important matters that need my immediate attention, and I can't be wasting any more of my time here."

I had little doubt his intent was to leave the uninitiated listener—like the reporter—with the impression that of the two of us, he was the more important attorney. The guy who had to be off to deal with something like a capital murder case he'd had to put on hold to deal with this inconvenient little trial.

But I also knew him well enough to suspect what was really so all-fired important was a Johnny Walker Red Label Tall he knew could be poured somewhere other than where we were standing.

Either way, we were done, and so we left for home.

The following day, the paper carried the story. Below the headline was a byline that read,

Noted Defense Counsel P. Cummings says the Case Was Shakespearian—Much Ado About Nothing.

I read the whole article all the way through, then reread it. Not a single thing I'd said to the reporter about the case or its dismissal had found its way into his narrative. Beyond quoting Cummings, the article was merely a recitation of the facts of the case, the district attorney's motion to dismiss, and the fact that it was dismissed. So far as the reporter was concerned, even printing my name as the other attorney on the case would apparently have been a waste of ink.

A few weeks later, I ran into Cummings again in the courthouse hallway.

"Hey, Kiddo. How you doing?"

"Great. And you?"

"Great. Couldn't be better, Kiddo."

"I saw your quote about Shakespeare in the paper. That was a stroke of genius. Congrats."

"Yeah. That was sweet, wasn't it? Sorry, Kiddo, you probably should have gotten more credit than the paper gave you after all the work you did. But that's the way it goes. Look at it this way. At least you learned that reporters are just like you and me. They want life to be simple so they can do their job and get back home by nightfall to screw the pooch or whatever else it is they may like to do. They don't want legal theory or messy facts. They just want a sound bite. Remember that and your life will also be made that much simpler when you have to deal with those guys."

"Got it. You're probably right. Good to know," I responded. "One other question. I looked in the court's file and saw your bill. How is it even possible that your bill on the case was a $1,000 more than mine?"

Without blinking, he replied, "Oh, I basically did that for you, Kiddo. I wanted you to get paid for all the work you did. For that to happen, the judge who has to sign off on those things had to feel the amount you billed was reasonable. The only way I could see that happening was for my bill to exceed yours, demonstrating that you as the junior attorney on the case were billing them a lesser amount than the lead attorney on the case—me."

"Huh? Lead attorney?"

"Don't worry, Kiddo. I was right, wasn't I? They paid your bill, didn't they?"

"Yes. They did pay it."

"Told you, Kiddo. Like I always say, in the end, it all works out just fine. It always does."

"I guess so."

"You gotta learn to trust me, Kiddo. By the way in case I didn't tell you before, you did a great job on that case. Good work. I hope we can work together again sometime soon."

"Me too."

"See ya, Kiddo."

With that, he walked out of the courthouse and out of my life. If I had to guess, he was heading to lunch somewhere that would let him get his mid-day dose of smokes and Johnnie Walker Red Label Talls with maybe a sandwich on the side.

As he left, I could not avoid the thought that in one sense

he *had* been correct. The whole experience I'd just been through with him had certainly left me in possession of more wisdom and experience than I had before he'd entered my life.

In the end, what did that make him? A wise man or a fool?

Maybe a little of both? Then again, perhaps that described me too. Or perhaps it is a description of all of us who have been given both the blessing and the curse of living out our lives here in a broken world.

Looking back on all of it now, of one thing I am sure. God used Cummings to pivot my professional life toward a new direction every bit as much as God had tried to use Savannah Georgia Booth to pivot my spiritual life years before.

Looking back on all of it now, of one thing I am sure.

God used both the wisdom and the foolishness of P. Cummings to make me a better man.

I learned I could do the work to handle a complicated case like the one we'd just finished.

I learned that people's reputations don't always mirror their character.

I learned that things often do work out as they're supposed to, but just as often may not.

I learned to remember when talking to a reporter that like most of us they just want to get through the day and make their job as easy as they can.

And at the end of the day, one major result of God putting P. Cummings in my life in the case of Brock M. was that I was no longer a newbie in the world of criminal defense.

Looking back now, what I regret most about my dealings with Cummings is that it never occurred to me to discuss with him even the little I knew about God at that time in my life.

Not long after we parted that day in the courthouse hallway, he went out to dinner with his wife, gave the waitress their order, then got up to run back out to his car for a pack of cigarettes he'd left behind.

"I'll be right back, Kiddo," he told his wife.

But this time he was wrong. On his way back across the parking lot, a heart attack dropped him to the ground deader than a doornail.

On the bright side, at least he had been allowed to die with his boots on. Then again, he hadn't gotten to touch the Johnny Walker Red Label Tall he'd left behind on the table where his wife was now sitting alone waiting for him to return.

Given these circumstances, I have wondered from time to time whether if I'd been there and he'd been able to, would he still have smiled and told me one last time, "Like I've always told you, Kiddo, it all works out just fine in the end."

In the end, perhaps this time he never knew it hadn't.

And who knows whether he [is] ... a wise man or a fool? Yet he will have control over all the fruit of my labor for which I have labored by acting wisely under the sun. This too is vanity.[2]

Keep your way far from her and do not go near her house ... or you will give your vigor to others and your years to the cruel one.[1]

~

16

THE ONE NIGHT STAND

Warning: this chapter contains graphic material.

As I mentioned in the last chapter, by the time I came across his path, Brock M. was twenty-eight years old with a list of prior arrests as long as my arm. His well-muscled height, good looks, and shock of blonde hair projected a wholesome All-American look. That is, except for the charcoal-gray prison tattoos covering both forearms.

A detective told me once that prison tats were typically colorless—like the lives their wearers led. They were gray because ground-up pencil lead mixed with water was the only ink available in prison. He also told me that for law enforcement such tattoos were like a convict I.D. card since they enabled police to immediately identify those with a prison background when encountered on the outside.

"They might as well put a tattoo on their foreheads that reads Former Prison Inmate," the detective concluded.

For me, Brock's tattoos simply affirmed what I already knew from his paperwork. I just mentally absorbed their existence as prima facie visual evidence that his brain might be operating on the wattage of a dull bulb. Even so, I wanted to give him the benefit of the doubt until I got to know him a little better. Reserving judgment was a courtesy I tried to extend to all clients I met in lockup. In Brock's case, as already indicated, he kind of surprised me. Even in the dour, depressing, and sterile atmosphere of a county jail interview room, he'd had no problem presenting himself as a cheerful, even a humorous individual.

This suggested to me that Brock was either a man with some intelligence or crazy. As was also my practice, I kept open to the possibility he could be a bit of both. Past experience told me guys like Brock rarely fit into the category of "what you first see is what you get."

As we became more acquainted, I was able to determine that when Brock was not locked up, his numerous priors rendered him for all practical purposes unemployable. So he was usually broke. Which steered him toward the path by which he would inevitably arrive at his next arrest. For those reasons alone, anyone getting to know him well soon found that despite a façade of cheerful humor, he could also be sullen and angry. And when pushed—which didn't take much as I learned by the end of our acquaintance—even dangerous.

This was the Brock M. who had walked into a local bar on the prowl several months before we met. That night he'd been looking for an opportunity to make some money as much as for some cheap sex. From his point of view, he'd be happy if he came across either. It wasn't long before he stumbled on what he thought might be a chance to get both.

When he spotted her, Loretta R. was already seated alone at the bar that ran almost the whole length of the room. It wasn't too busy yet, so Brock wound his way past some empty tables to belly up to the bar. Except for a few dim lights overhead, the room was kept dark to minimize the defects of a generally far-less-than-perfect-looking clientele. By comparison, brighter lights illuminated dozens of bottles of every sort of booze imaginable lined up on shelves behind the bar as though beckoning customers to sidle up and order a drink.

But Brock had a different agenda. A single glance had told him that Loretta was a woman with all the right curves and just the right attitude. As he put it to me in the course of our first conversation, "She was a woman who had come dressed for business in such a way that everybody in the saloon would know just why she was there, if you know what I mean."

Needless to say, it didn't take long for them to start up a conversation and discover they had much in common—their age, blonde hair, good looks, and hope for sex that night—along with a mutual love of methamphetamines, which they both agreed made the "chemistry" of any evening better. It was starting to look like a match made somewhere clearly other than heaven—for that one night at least. After all, even if it didn't work out in the long run, how bad could it be so long as the supply of meth held out and the sex was good?

And apparently it was pretty good in the beginning. That is, according to Brock. When Loretta took him home that night, she hadn't yet told him anything about her inconvenient four-year-old daughter, parked with a friend for the evening. Somewhat along the lines of what's good for the goose should be good for the gander, Brock also failed to mention that he'd only recently been released from a stretch in state prison. That was even before getting to the fact that the conditions of Brock's parole were being violated by being in that bar in search of meth in the first place.

But those were details that could be sorted out later. Neither wanted such technicalities to get in the way of advancing their mutual hormone-and-drug-based agenda. As Brock saw it, beyond just getting lucky, a meth user like Loretta offered him the possibility of turning her into a future customer or a prospective supplier. Either presented the opportunity to put some cash in his pocket if he played it right.

In the following weeks, both Brock and Loretta were happy. He was charming, and she was accommodating. As long as the sex and the drugs remained in good supply, they both chose to let the good times keep rolling. Notwithstanding the return of her daughter to Loretta's mobile home, Brock quickly became more than just a one-nighter and soon after moved in with the two of them.

The detective's report supporting Brock's indictment for child molestation indicated he had told the detective during his interview, "Loretta's daughter was a pretty sweet kid. She mostly kept to herself and didn't bother us. That is, unless she was hungry, dirty, tired, or something along those lines. You know how kids can be, right?"

After several months, the honeymoon period of the couple's relationship began to unravel. Loretta put it to the detective this way: "It began with arguments over little things. Like Brock failing to pay his share for the rent, groceries, and his drug habit. But over time the arguments grew worse. Turns out he really was just a free-loading %#&."

According to Brock, he was the one who finally decided he couldn't take it anymore. He'd long before concluded Loretta was crazy and so not worthy of his standing on ceremony to end their relationship. One day he just took off without notice, sincerely hoping to never look back.

A reason perhaps closer to the truth could be that Brock's instincts were telling him to get out before anything happened that might be grounds for his parole officer to return him to prison. Like the neighbors calling 911 to report domestic violence next door. Which in turn might lead to the discovery of Brock's recreational use of Loretta's meth, most certainly stowed somewhere in her mobile home.

Still, Brock's version left me—and evidently the investigating detective—wondering whether his reasons for the sudden departure might not also include putting distance between himself and the place where he had just sexually molested a child. According to Loretta's initial version, he had fled from her home only after she'd called the sheriff's department. Not for anything connected with her daughter, but for Brock not paying his part of the rent and groceries. She seemed to feel the deputies might help collect the debt Brock owed her.

Of course she didn't quite word it like that, or the deputies would never have bothered to follow up. Once the officers were at her door, the story she told included Brock stealing money, repeatedly beating her, and taking drugs that were his with a minor in the house. Any one of which was sufficient to instigate an arrest given Brock's parolee status.

There was one minor detail she didn't bother to mention to the initial responding officers, as the detective who later interviewed Loretta noted. In her words, "Oh, I might have forgotten to say anything about Brock sexually abusing my daughter. If so, I'm sorry and I'm telling you now because he's a dangerous %o#&! and should be locked up."

The detective undoubtedly suspected she might have added this tidbit out of spite. But it was enough to have Brock arrested post haste.

Brock was sleeping in a cheap flophouse in a bleak industrial part of town when a horde of deputies came busting through his door, flashlights and assault rifles all directed at Brock, who was lying face-down asleep on the bed. As they yelled at Brock to stay on his stomach and keep both hands in sight, an officer's knee pressed down on the base of his neck to keep him pinned while he was handcuffed.

Unfortunately for Brock, but perhaps even more unfortunately for Loretta, before they could read Brock his rights to remain silent, Brock spontaneously spouted off, "Hey guys, I know what this is all about. That skank Loretta called you guys, didn't she? Well, let me tell you, she's is a lying meth-queen slut. She can't be trusted for %#&!. She's probably saying I owe her money, but I don't owe her %#!&. She's pissed because I dropped her like a bad habit, and she's just doing this to me to get even."

Was he hoping he could convince the deputies that arresting him was just a big mistake and that the SWAT team members now crowding the room would just leave him alone so he could go back to sleep? If so, he was wrong.

He'd likely have made a very different response to the arresting SWAT members if he'd known what Loretta had already told the detective about Brock's sexual molestation of her daughter. Things like Brock getting so mad about her daughter's crying that he'd hung the little girl by her T-shirt on a hook in the kitchen, then pushed a broomstick up between the child's legs, screaming, "This is what your mommy likes. How about you? Does this make you happy, too? Maybe now you'll shut the %#&! up!"

Perhaps Loretta thought her version would gain the

detective's empathy for her and her daughter and that the hammer of justice would only impact Brock.

If so, she was also wrong.

When she got Brock arrested, she probably hadn't anticipated that he would denounce her to the deputies as a meth-queen. Or maybe she wasn't aware of the maxim often applied by detectives investigating child abuse that meth use and sexual molestation of young children often go hand-in-hand. She clearly didn't anticipate that the detective would use the differing versions of their breakup to obtain a warrant to search her home for drugs—which, not surprisingly, they found.

So much to her surprise, about the same time she'd arranged to have Brock arrested, the detective also had Loretta arrested for the use and possession of illegal narcotics as well as child endangerment. As a consequence, her daughter was taken from her by child protective services. All of which eventually led to the arrest of her meth supplier, who would soon find himself represented by none other than the renowned P. Cummings.

So it was that the detective's findings were all wrapped up in the common criminal complaint filed against the three of them for the various felonies each was alleged to have committed. Off to court they went, beginning the next phase of a relationship originally intended to be a one-night stand. For the next few months at least, their "dates" would be brief, presumably drug-free, and only occur while standing together in court.

By the time I came on the scene, Loretta's parents had retained private counsel to represent her. I've already told how Cummings maneuvered me into the representing the "bad guy" among the three defendants. Brock had been charged with nine separate felony counts, including his alleged use, possession, and sale of narcotics, aggravated assault with bodily injury, and the sexual molestation of a minor. In total, charges that exposed him to over one hundred years in state prison if he was convicted.

To say the least, that's an expensive date!

Brock's situation was not a matter to be taken lightly by anyone, much less by either Brock or me. Nor was it. It soon became apparent that the district attorney assigned to the case was out for blood. And, because of the horrid nature of the crimes alleged, so was the press.

Over the months following their joint arraignment, an abundance of caution and attention to detail were the watchwords of the day guiding our journey toward trial. The problem the prosecution faced was that Loretta's daughter was too young to admit or deny much of anything with unimpeachable certainty. After taking protective custody of the child, the social workers involved had photographed some redness in her vaginal area. But many explanations for a little girl's redness other than sexual molestation could be offered in defense. In Brock's favor were also a lack of seminal discharge or any other evidence of a vaginal assault.

In the end, the case ultimately came down to Loretta's word against Brock's, and neither could lay claim to more credibility than the other. Moreover, as joint defendants in the same case, each had to be very careful of how they testified, as anything they said could present a two-edged sword that could hurt their own defense.

To boost the odds in favor of his own case, the district attorney met on the side out of court with Loretta's attorney to work out a plea deal. Loretta ultimately agreed to plead guilty to one drug-related felony for a sentence of two-and-a-half years in state prison. One benefit of this deal was that it dropped the child abuse charges, crucial if Loretta was to have any hope of regaining custody of her child once she got out of prison. But the deal was contingent, of course, upon Loretta's willingness to testify at trial against both Brock and Cummings' client.

The plea deal did not bode well for Brock, but he didn't seem to care. From his perspective, nothing had changed. Everything Loretta had said about domestic abuse, stealing money, or his use of the meth found in her residence was a lie. He hadn't stolen anything, the red marks on her daughter were probably just some kind of rash, and the meth was Loretta's, not his. She'd only told the detectives these lies to get back at him for leaving her. In essence, he was guilty of nothing, and any reasonable person—like presumably any random juror—could only agree he should be set free.

That doubts about Brock's version of reality remained in both my mind and others would be an understatement. As the days, weeks, and months of our pre-trial preparations went by, his behavior left little question that his true nature had the potential to be more frighteningly dangerous than first impressions might suggest.

Suffice it to say that over time I became increasingly

glad for the thick Plexiglas barrier separating us in the interview room. On any particular day, I had to guess whether he was angry with the system, Loretta, the fact he was still in custody, or just with me. Probably all of the preceding reasons were true at different points in time. It was enough to make anyone leery of him.

No doubt the court bailiffs felt the same. Especially after he tried at one of his court appearances to orchestrate a unified effort with his fellow inmates in the court's holding cell to overthrow the guards in lockup. The plan was to attack the next time a guard opened the door to retrieve a prisoner, then make a mass escape.

What Brock didn't know was that a hidden microphone allowed the deputies in lockup to listen to his attempt to rally the troops. So it should surprise no one to learn that Brock was the next one called to come out of lockup, upon which the guards shackled together virtually all visible appendages so that if anyone escaped pursuant to Brock's "plan," it would not include him. That is how he appeared in court up to the day of jury selection when the chains were exchanged for the electrocution vest.

I was never able to verify Brock's later complaint that he'd been tortured upon his return to county jail the night after his escape attempt. According to his story, to punish him for even thinking about escaping, they'd brought him to a small room in the basement, stripped him naked, and chained him to a metal chair. Then they'd turned the air conditioning on full blast, directed a single bright light at his face, and left him there to freeze with no sleep all night long and most of the next day.

One problem with trying to bring such a complaint to the court's attention was that the alleged torture would leave no lasting physical evidence other than Brock possibly getting a cold. Nor was a judge likely to take the word of a defendant like Brock over that of the guards, who would of course deny it ever happened. Not to mention, as I pointed out to Brock, the genuine possibility that accusing the guards of such a miscreant and illegal misadventure might result in further and even worse miscreant and illegal misadventures.

Brock got the point and quickly agreed to drop his complaint about the torture. But that didn't stop the bailiffs from inconveniencing him with an abundance of chains for the balance of our pre-trial court appearances.

Over time, things like this led me to realize that the question of whether or not he actually *did* the crimes he'd been charged with was distinctly different from the question of whether or not he was *capable* of doing the horrendous things he was accused of. But such thoughts did nothing to deter me from providing him the best defense he was entitled to under the law.

I can't speak for other criminal defense attorneys, but over the years I've often found myself being asked, "How can a lawyer who is a Christian like you justify defending people like Brock?"

My first thought when asked this question was that there went a person who had probably never experienced being falsely accused by the "system." If they had, they wouldn't be asking that question. Especially if they'd ever had to face serious penalties attached to the outcome of any due process they might have been afforded to determine the "truth."

At the beginning of my criminal defense practice, I usually tried to answer this question with a short spiel about everybody's constitutional right to due process. But as my practice developed, so did my grounding in my faith. This led to my answer to this question becoming more, shall we say, refined.

As mentioned earlier, by this point I had renewed my church attendance. My participation in the ancillary Bible studies allowed me to in time appreciate more fully that all of us as human beings are broken individuals in some way or another, much like P. Cummings and me, not to mention guys like Brock. As such, the Bible declares that we are all in need of an intercessor to advocate for us before God to refute the accusations of Satan, who left unrestrained and to his own devices would have us all condemned and banished from heaven for eternity for the sins we've all committed.

So if that applies to all of us, who are any of us to say that people like Brock should not be afforded a defense in our courts? Especially considering that the precision with which they mete out justice falls at the very least far short of heavenly standards. In fact, too much of the time it's like a physician attempting to do brain surgery using a meat cleaver instead of a scalpel.

That said, I must admit Brock's case did leave me wondering from time to time what might happen to the next little girl he encountered if by perchance the criminal justice system failed to arrive at the *truth*—whatever that *truth* may be.

That was the thought beginning to coalesce in my mind even before I received the call.

The lips of a harlot drip honey and smoother than oil is her speech;
but in the end she is bitter as wormwood, sharp as a two-edged sword.
Her feet go down to death.[2]

Be ... on the alert. Your adversary, the devil, prowls around like a
roaring lion, seeking someone to devour.[1] *Therefore submit to God,*
resist the devil and he will flee from you.[2]

17

WHAT EVIL IS

Warning: this chapter contains
graphic material.

Nearly eleven months after the case began, all counsel—i.e., the district attorney, Cummings, and me—were finally able to agree with the judge that no further delays were necessary. He then set the trial date and referred us to the distant court that would actually handle the trial. All of which revived the local paper's interest in the crimes. Case details and the date of the upcoming trial made the front page.

This in turn led to my office getting a call from a man who had seen the article and wanted to talk to me about the case. He identified himself as a relative of Brock but refused to say what exactly he was calling about, only that it was important and related to Brock and the upcoming trial.

Thinking he might have something new and helpful—like evidence of an alibi or Brock's good character—I accepted his request to meet in person at my office. But an alarm was going off in my mind. For one thing, if what he had to say was so important and secret, why had he waited so long after Brock's arrest to come forward?

The only time he would come to the office was Saturday, and I didn't particularly like that either. My staff would be gone, so he and I would be alone. This brought risk to the deal, if for no other reason than that he'd said he was Brock's relative. Which might not be a good thing from what I already knew of Brock. Whatever happened at the meeting, it would be his word against mine if things went south. Still, it didn't seem like I had a choice.

The man turned out to be Brock's half-brother. Funny how dirty fingernails, wrinkled clothes, and unkempt hair can affect how we evaluate another person. My first impression was that while I didn't dislike him, that wouldn't be too hard to do if I gave it just a bit of time and effort.

The man was obviously nervous, which caused me to start feeling even more cautious than I already was. He began by telling me he knew his half-brother well but didn't know if what he had to say was appropriate or even legal. Well, frankly, neither did I until I could get out of him precisely what that was. Which left me no option except to tell him to go ahead.

He hunched forward in his chair and leaned in toward my desk. His narrowed eyes looked directly into mine as he asked, "Do you think it's all right for me to say you aren't doing anyone any favor by trying to help Brock any more than you absolutely have to?"

"What do you mean by that?" I responded.

He hesitated, looking down at his lap as though contemplating the presence of an oil spot on his jeans. Then he said in the slow, measured cadence of a timid child, "Some people are best to be in prison for the sake of everyone concerned. I guess I'm here to let you know that, so far as his own family is concerned, Brock is that kind of a guy."

The immediate questions jumping to my mind were whether the guy simply didn't want Brock showing up at family reunions or whether he and possibly his extended family actually feared Brock. Did he know something specific about whether or not Brock had done the ugly things he was being accused of doing to that little girl? Or was it a combo of these possibilities?

Before I could ask him, he shook his head. "That's all I had. I've said all I'm going to say. Just know this. As far as everybody who knows him is concerned, it's better that Brock stays locked up. So I'm here to ask you not to try too hard to get him out."

With that, he got up, thanked me for listening, and left my office without even shaking my hand. I never saw the man again, but he'd done nothing to modify the impression I'd formed by now that Brock was not a good guy for anybody to be around for very long. It also did nothing to answer the question of whether Brock did or did not actually sexually abuse a four-year-old little girl. Still, the visit from Brock's half-brother left me unsettled, with that question now spinning around in my brain as though on steroids.

A few days later, it looked more likely that Brock's half-brother might get his wish. I received a call from the district attorney handling the case. I could almost feel his smug smile coming through the phone as he reminded me that Loretta had pleaded guilty to one drug-related felony in exchange for testifying at trial against Brock. Since he was well aware that I already knew this, I guessed it wasn't the sole purpose of his call. I quickly learned that I was correct. He went on to ask whether my client had thought any more about the plea agreement his office had offered him a few months before.

Let me stop here a minute to explain that plea deals are interesting beasts in the field of criminal law. Some people may think of them as ways for hardened criminals to get lesser sentences because the district attorney or judge or both are too lenient to prosecute them. In practice, the plea deal game is more akin to the defense counsel playing poker with the district attorney.

In cases where defendants are most likely guilty, but the district attorney knows the case has flaws, a plea deal provides for at least some measure of justice to be meted out while avoiding the risk of losing at trial and allowing a guilty man to go completely free. Exactly how much incarceration time the district attorney can exact depends on how flawed the case is and to what degree the defense counsel may either know about those weaknesses or be able to leverage them to his client's advantage. Needless to say, the game can include a whole lot of posturing, bluffing, and guessing by attorneys on both sides of the deal.

But there are also situations involving defendants who have been wrongly accused. To them, plea deals can be a devil's snare they feel they can't afford to avoid. For instance, take a guy who is looking at over a hundred years in prison if he loses at trial. Even an innocent person finding himself in that position might decide an offer of ten years seems pretty good. At least they can see the light of day at the end instead of the dark abyss of no return from what could be a life sentence based on a roll of the dice in front of a jury. Whether they accept the plea deal or not depends on their calculation of the risks attending a trial and the individual defendant's personal tolerance for such risk.

People hear all the time about a trial being a crapshoot in so far as how it may turn out. But few are called upon to carefully consider this possibility more than defendants looking at long sentences. It is they who are made most aware that the crapshoot might not work out so well for them. Do they take the deal and have the hope of seeing daylight or turn it down and play for keeps?

Again, this depends largely on the risk tolerance—i.e., courage—of the individual defendant. That is to say, not all innocent defendants would make the same decision under identical circumstances. Some will have the temerity to stand on principle and refuse to plead to something they didn't do. These are the people I tend to admire.

Others, even though innocent, will choose to take the deal to avoid the risk of a possibly horrible outcome at trial. The best example might be a young man wrongfully accused of inappropriate sexual battery by some irate or scorned neighborhood girl. If a jury believes her, he could not only be looking at a felony conviction and prison but having to register as a sexual offender every place he lives for the rest of his life. So when offered a deal that includes pleading to a misdemeanor non-sexual battery in exchange for one year in the county jail with no registration requirement attached, even an innocent person might rationally choose to accept such a deal. These are the people I tend to completely understand and sympathize with.

Added to the mix of this emotional cauldron are the defense attorney's professional skills coupled with his or her own personal character traits, which can range from being totally risk-averse to stupidly courageous to completely indifferent. Simply put, some attorneys will do anything to avoid a trial and will steer clients into accepting deals that may not be in their best interests. Others want the notches of trials added to their reputation belt and will steer the client in the opposite direction toward trial. Others will take it to trial just because it pays more, notwithstanding the risks to the client.

In one instance of this latter variety, I once watched a judge sentence a man to life in prison who—in my opinion —should never have gone to trial. The trial fee had apparently been something the defense attorney couldn't bring himself to pass up. So he'd persuaded his client to decline the plea deal the district attorney had offered.

When the judge finished with the sentencing, the client turned to his attorney with tears in his eyes and a redness of face that screamed his present state of shock muddled with quite understandable fear.

"What are we going to do next?" he asked.

In response, the attorney stood up, put his hands together in front of him, then pretended to swing an imaginary nine-iron as he said to the shock of even the hardened bailiff, "I don't know what you have planned, my man. But I think I'll take the afternoon off and go play some golf."

With that, he packed his briefcase and left the court without even looking back at his client, who was being scuttled out the back way by deputies, never to be seen again.

I tell you all this about plea deals to give you a better understanding of how it is entirely possible for innocent people to be locked up. And to let you know why—within this matrix of emotional paradoxes at the core of high stakes plea deals—I told the D.A. I'd get back to him if Brock's refusal to accept his plea deal had changed.

Brock had been offered a sentence in state prison for approximately ten years in exchange for his guilty plea to one count of aggravated battery upon a child. All other charges would be dismissed. Personally, I thought he might want to seriously consider taking it. Ten years was far less than the hundred-plus years he could be looking at if convicted at trial. At worst, he'd be getting out around thirty-nine years of age or possibly earlier if he racked up enough good behavior/half-time credits while locked up. In my view, it was a deal that would leave him enough life left to get on with it once he got out.

But the final decision was up to Brock, and he'd

turned the plea deal down once already. The question now was whether he'd hold to that course once he was reminded of the potential hurricane named Loretta headed our way whose testimony could have a devastating impact on the outcome of his case. So the next day I drove to the central inmate holding facility where Brock had taken up residence for much of the past year.

As it turned out, the trip was a long one for nothing. Brock again refused the deal. From what I could decipher, his rationale involved one or more of the three following possible reasons.

First, he continued to maintain that he was not guilty.

Second, Loretta was a lying %o#&!, and he was confident no jury would believe anything she said.

Third, if he did take the plea and go to prison, he would surely be killed by some inmate in a prison population that, generally speaking, has an extremely low tolerance for anyone accused of sexually abusing a child.

Which of these three reasons held most sway in bringing Brock to his decision, I'll never know. All I did know was that two of the three possible reasons were pretty persuasive even for me. So I informed the district attorney. Less than a month later, jury selection was completed, and the trial was about to begin.

As mentioned, a delay was requested by the district attorney on the morning opening statements were to be made. As we all waited outside in the hallway, I spotted the district attorney crouched down some distance along the corridor talking with a small girl. I could guess this was

Loretta's daughter. The woman beside her was most likely her social worker.

After a few minutes, the district attorney stood up. He said a few words to the social worker, then re-entered the court. A minute or so later, the bailiff came out and told Cummings and me to come back in. As we walked back into the courtroom, I saw the little girl heading down the hall with her social worker.

With a look over at Cummings I asked, "What do you think that was all about?"

True to character, he replied, "Who knows, Kiddo? But one thing's pretty sure. Whatever it was, it's probably not very good for us. But I'll bet you one thing. We're just about to find out."

Ya think? I told myself. We resumed our places, and the deputies brought our shuffling clients in to resume theirs. The next step would be to seat the jury. But that was when the district attorney made his surprise announcement to dismiss all charges.

As the judge dismissed the case, I was simultaneously perplexed, relieved, and excited for Brock, not to mention myself. In my view, we had both dodged bullets that could have proved disastrous. Me by possibly losing a relatively well publicized case. Brock by possibly going to prison for the rest of his life. But even though we'd just avoided those respective fates, Brock still remained furious.

Still swearing, Brock was led away to be returned to the central jail and from there to be processed for release. I probably should have just left well enough alone and gone home. But I couldn't bring myself to do it. On some level, I think I wanted to revel at least a little with my client over this fortuitous outcome before rejoining Cummings for our road trip home.

So after talking for a few minutes with the district attorney and judge, I told Cummings I would meet him in the hallway in a few minutes. Then I went back to the lockup and requested a moment with my client.

At best, the court's lockup room was dimly lit. Perhaps that was to keep inmates calm, or maybe the county didn't consider the kind of people staying there worth paying for more electricity. Who knows! As my eyes adjusted to the gloom, I told the deputy I'd like to see my client. He responded with a glum nod toward one of the holding cells.

I took from this that the deputy was not as thrilled with my client's dismissal as I was. Then again, lockup deputies are not known for their geniality. So I just headed across the room to look for Brock. I found him standing in the center of his cell with his back to me.

In reality, the holding cells could more accurately be described as cages. Each ten-foot by ten-foot space was backed onto a cement wall. The three remaining sides consisted of an iron mesh similar to heavy-gauge chain link fencing that extended from floor to the ceiling. A single bulb well out of reach above Brock's head offered faint illumination. He'd already changed from his borrowed civilian clothing into his orange jail "pajamas" in preparation for transport back to the central jail.

"Brock, you all right?" I asked as I approached. "Congratulations! By tonight you're going to be a free man."

As I spoke, Brock just stood there silently without making any effort to turn around to face me. Then he began talking right over me with a low-voiced growl I'd never before heard from him. It was a deep, guttural sound like something emanating from a predatory beast. In a word, it sounded *eerie.*

"I'm going to sue you, you %#&!!" he seethed. "And I'm also going to sue the judge. I'm going to sue the district attorney. And I'm going to particularly enjoy suing the #@*% sheriffs."

As he continued, the pitch of his rant continued to rise, "Do you hear me? I'm going to sue all of you %#&!."

Incredulous, I could only ask, "What are you talking about, Brock? Did you not hear what happened out there? You're getting set free today. That's a helluva lot better than Loretta got. She folded for two-and-a-half years in state prison. She's not getting out anytime soon, but you are!"

"I don't give a flying %#&! about Loretta!" he yelled. "I told all of you twelve months ago it was a pack of lies, and what did I get? I've been tortured. I've been kept in a cage. %#&! all of you and your mothers! I'm suing the bunch of you for millions. You hear me? When I get done, I'll own all of you!"

By now his voice had risen to a guttural scream. Only when his tirade reached peak volume did he turn around to face me for the first time. His turn was chillingly slow. The single bulb above him created long, creepy shadows on his face as it came in to my view, casting in darkness the sockets where his eyes and mouth should have been.

But that was not the only reason the blood drained from my head at that moment. As he continued to turn, something else made me want to run and escape the room in which I now felt as though I was being held against my will—Brock's turgid penis emerging through the opening flap of his orange jailhouse pajamas. The total image staring me in the face had all the appearance of the demonic—pure evil. If you are shocked by this, be assured, so was I.

My head was spinning, and I felt almost faint as an undeniable reality crashed into my mind like a sledge hammer.

It wasn't Brock's anger.

It wasn't his erection.

It wasn't his screaming that he was going to %#&! us all.

It was the combination of all these things in context of the pure evil I was witnessing. Maybe Brock hadn't done the specific evil they'd accused him of. But he most certainly was a beast who *could* have done it. And only now was he completely revealing himself to be someone who very well *might* have.

In that instant, I knew beyond any doubt that his furious anger when coupled with his unbridled sense of power over others—like he was experiencing now and perhaps with Loretta's daughter hanging from a hook in the kitchen—was for Brock an aphrodisiac.

Whether or not he'd done the crimes the court had dismissed just moments before, I knew with a chilling certainty that a serious crime against humanity was about to happen when this man was again put out on the street to roam freely among us.

With his venomous rant still ringing in my ears, I left the room without a further word to find Cummings and go home. Nausea rose up within me. I needed to get some fresh air. But mostly I needed to get back to somewhere I could replace the darkness I was in with some light.

Cummings may have been right in one sense. Perhaps Brock's case had been Shakespearean. But in another sense, he'd been very wrong that day he spoke to the press.

For many months that followed, the words of Brock's half-brother echoed in my mind alongside horrifying visions of a terrified little girl hanging from a hook in a kitchen inches from the hot breath of a vicious man with a hard-on like the one I had seen. So far as I was concerned, the nightmare that had followed upon Brock's one-night-stand was not then nor ever would be *Much Ado About Nothing*.

In truth, the newspaper headline that next day after Brock's release should have been a warning to the local populace such as:

Much Ado About the Existence of Evil in this World that Roams Freely Among Us All Like a Roaring Lion Seeking to Devour.

But he who listens to me shall live securely, and will be at ease from the dread of evil.[3]

The way of the wicked is like darkness; they do not know over what they stumble.[1]

~

18

SHOULD A MURDER MATTER?

L ong after the last time I saw Brock, I was called in by Judge Hewitt's clerk to represent a man named Darryl. Among other things, Darryl had been charged with robbery involving the use of a firearm. Since he had a prior felony conviction, he was looking at a decade minimum in state prison and quite possibly much longer due to the sentencing enhancements that come with the use of a firearm in the commission of a violent felony.

Before interviewing my new client, I stopped by the courtroom to pick up the complaint and sheriff's report. The district attorney on duty that day was already laying his files out on his table for the morning arraignments.

Without looking up, he informed me, "On your guy, we're offering ten years on one count of armed robbery. We'll drop the other charges and gun enhancements and make the time he'd have to serve on his prior felony conviction run concurrent with this sentence."

Not knowing anything about the case yet, I nodded

with a smile. "Thanks. I'll let him know and get back to you."

As I left the courtroom, I made a note of the offer. *Hmmm, ten years state prison. They must have a fairly solid case against this guy. Well, we'll see soon enough.*

As I approached the lockup window, I called my client's name out to the bailiff, who was seated at a desk beyond a metal screen. The name echoed down an unseen passage as it was relayed from officer to officer until it reached the unseen officer who would move my new client from his holding cell to the interview room.

Before long, Darryl joined me. A tall, thin, good-looking black man about thirty years old, he was dressed in a standard-issue short-sleeved orange jumpsuit. This was accessorized by chains that hobbled his ankles as well as handcuffs attached to another chain locked around his waist.

The deputy unfastened one of the cuffs so Darryl could pick up the phone to talk with me. I gestured for him to take a seat and we began.

"How you doing?" I asked.

"How would you be doing if you were me?" he responded. "I hate this place."

That I could understand. Painted an ugly brown-beige, the cement walls of the narrow cubicle were cold to the touch and lit on each side only by a single naked bulb dangling above us. Certainly nothing in the décor was intended to promote either the hope or comfort of anyone who found themselves seated here. In fact, now that he'd mentioned it, the whole setup was downright depressing and bleak. If I badly wanted out of here, how badly must people like Darryl who couldn't leave?

I started skimming through the detective's report to get a feel for the evidence against my client, then cut to the chase. "What can you tell me about how you came to be here?"

"Listen," Darryl said, "When you finish reading the report, you're going to see they got me. I'm on video. There was a camera in the store I didn't know about. Besides that, there are two witnesses I know of, maybe more. It was a stupid thing to do, I admit. But that's not what I want to talk to you about right now. I don't want to go back to the joint. And I want to deal."

"Deal? What with?"

"Bro, I got something they're going to want more than me. And I'll do a trade."

"Okay, so make this simple for me. What exactly are you talking about?"

"I've got a videotape they're going to want. And I'll give it to them if they let me go on this case."

"Okay, tell me more. What's on the video that would make them want to even think about letting you go on an armed robbery? It would have to be pretty good."

"It is. It's a video of a murder the cops haven't solved yet."

"Really? Do tell. How do you know they haven't solved it?"

"Because the guy who did it has never been arrested."

"Did what?"

"Killed my friend, bro! He shot him. Shot him dead

only a few feet away from me."

"So did you know the shooter?"

"Yeah, I know him. And since I shot the video, he's been out doing business as usual."

"So was this murder recent?"

"About a year ago out at a cabin where my buddy lived."

"And how did you come by the video?"

"I took the video."

"What?!?"

"Let me explain. I had just got out of prison and had nowhere else to go. My buddy was letting me stay with him until I could make some money."

"Okay, this isn't making sense. Please tell me you didn't help this guy shoot your buddy."

"No! Are you crazy? But the video shows who did."

"So how were you involved? You do realize that if you were with the shooter you're as guilty of murder in the eyes of the law as if you'd shot the guy yourself. You might want to think twice before you go there. And if you weren't with the shooter, why would he let you watch, much less videotape it, and live?"

"Look, just let me explain. My buddy was known to be a loner. This cabin he was letting me crash at was out in the desert in the middle of nowhere. I liked that—no neighbors and no cops."

"I got it. No neighbors. No cops. So no problems."

"You got it. For me, it was perfect. But my buddy was also known to be a pretty good source for meth and cocaine, if you know what I mean. And for years his source for all that was this other guy. You know, like one level up the food chain."

"So where does this other guy fit in? I don't see what difference this makes."

"That's what I'm going to tell you. It was him. My friend's buddy. The guy up the food chain. He's the guy who shot my buddy! He's the guy who killed him!!!"

"Your buddy's buddy killed your buddy? Some buddy, huh?"

"Yeah, you can say that again."

"Okay, so do you know *why* the guy shot him?"

"No, I don't know. All I know is that one morning about sunrise this guy comes driving up to the house in his Mercedes with his wife."

"Hold on! Are you saying the shooter's wife was there too?"

"Yeah! In fact, when I looked out the window after their fight started, she was out of the car and standing right next to her husband."

"Wait! How do you know it was the guy's wife?"

"Like I told you, I know the guy who killed my friend. Well, I didn't really know him. I've just seen him around for years and know where he lives. Everybody who deals cocaine in this area does. He and his wife live in that yellow house on the hill just off the highway outside of town."

"The big yellow one near the Olympus Road exit?"

"Yeah, that's the one."

"Are you serious? I know the house you're talking about!"

"Yeah, everybody does. It's a big one and hard to miss.

But to answer your question, I'm as serious as a heart attack. The guy who lives there is the guy who shot my buddy. He's the biggest cocaine supplier in the area. You might say, he's at the wholesale level. And my buddy who got shot was in retail."

"Okay, so keep going. This guy who lives in the yellow house comes up to your buddy's house with his wife. Then what happened?"

"I was asleep in the cabin when I heard yelling. It woke me up, in fact. I could tell from the way they were yelling somebody was really pissed. So I got up real slow and crawled up to the window, just hoping it wasn't the cops. That's when I saw my friend and this other guy—I'll call him Mr. Big—arguing. Then I noticed Mr. Big has a gun in his hand and thought to myself, this isn't good. That's when I remembered my friend has a video camera on the shelf by his kitchen. So I thought it'd probably be good to video this thing for later in case they got physical."

By now Darryl had my attention. He went on, "Well, about the time I got back to the window with the camera and started filming, Mr. Big shoots my buddy four times in the chest. Then he comes up to stand over my friend lying on the ground and shoots him one more time in the head. Cold as ice like he'd just swatted a fly, Mr. Big gets back into the Mercedes with his wife and drives off."

He leaned in as though to emphasize his sincerity. "Dude, all of this is on film. I even got a clear shot of the license plate. That was luck, dude. Because after the shooting started, it scared the %#&! out of me. So I turned off the camera and crawled as fast as I could to hide under my buddy's bed. You know, in case they came in to search the cabin. In fact, I stayed under the bed for about an hour, just shaking I was so scared and listening to see if I could hear their car come back."

"So why do you think they *didn't* search the cabin?" I asked with some skepticism.

Darryl shrugged. "Like I said, everybody knew my friend was a loner. It probably never occurred to them anyone else was crazy enough to be staying there with him out in the middle of nowhere."

My client certainly seemed to have an answer for everything.

"So why didn't you take the tape to the police? Why do you still have it?"

Darryl shrugged again. "Two reasons. For one, insurance with Mr. Big if I ever got sideways with him. You got to get who this guy is. Like I told you, no cocaine comes into this area he doesn't have a piece of. And if he doesn't have a piece, then anyone else trying to sell it tends to disappear pretty quickly. Everybody knows he's a nasty guy. Like I said, even I knew who he was when I saw him out there, and I knew guys like that can get you hurt."

"And the second reason?"

"Simple! Insurance with the cops. I figured it would be a good ace up my sleeve if I ever got popped again. My personal Get Out of Jail Free card, if you know what I mean. And right about now, I'm hoping I was right. Why the %#&! else do you think I'm talking about it with you? I want to deal."

"So where's the tape now?"

"I got it somewhere safe, but I can get it to you if you need it. Just say the word and I'll have somebody I know pick it up and bring it to your office."

"No! You hang on to it for now." My head was whirling around all the legal issues Darryl had just laid in my lap. "Does some friend of yours have it?"

"No."

"Is the friend who would go get it male or female?"

"Female."

"Does she know where it is?"

"No. I'd have to tell her."

"Is it wherever you were living when they arrested you?"

"You think I'm crazy? No. I've got it somewhere safe and no one but me knows where that is."

"Good. Keep it that way. If I know where it is, or worse yet, take possession of it and the sheriffs find out, they may be able to get a court to compel me to turn it over, deal or no deal. The way it is now, I have only your word it even exists and I prefer it stay that way. In the meantime, let me see what I can do."

That's how we left the matter. Later that day after Darryl's arraignment, I left Judge Hewitt's court a bit perplexed as to how to proceed. I hadn't mentioned the tape yet to either the district attorney handling the case or to Judge Hewitt. It would be a gross understatement to say that I needed time to think this whole thing through before I told anyone.

A few days later, I finally approached the district attorney to discuss Darryl's proposition. In an abundance of caution, I gave no specifics as to location, date, or time of the murder, much less any of the identities of the shooter, his wife, or the victim. I kept the discussion basically to a video of a fairly recent local homicide that so far as I knew hadn't yet been solved.

The district attorney listened with a poker face until I'd finished. Then to my surprise, he abruptly concluded our meeting without asking me anything more, only saying he'd have someone from the sheriff's homicide department contact me. If they were interested, we could talk later.

This was disquieting to say the least. What was my client getting us into should negotiations with the homicide detail turn bad? Could I be compelled to assist a homicide detective to recover the tape without a deal? Where did my legal and ethical obligations and duties lie? To help a detective solve a crime or to help a client avoid prison? Could anything I might say to the detective be used in court against Darryl?

Or perhaps more importantly, against me? Would any failure to cooperate make Darryl or me an accessory after the fact to murder?

So many issues! Such muddy legal waters!

Little did I know at the time that these murky waters would soon get even murkier and teach me that evil can come in different flavors.

Indeed, the light of the wicked goes out....And his own scheme brings him down.[2]

In the work of his own hands the wicked is snared.[1]

~

19

SOMETIMES THE GOOD GO BAD

When Detective Morgan called, I was as guarded as I had been with the district attorney, couching everything in the form of a hypothetical. In fact, as the conversation proceeded, I had a growing sense of descending further and further down a hypothetical rabbit hole, if not an abyss. Our conversation went a bit like this:

Detective: "Hello sir. My name is Detective Morgan. I'm with the sheriff's homicide detail. I was asked by the district attorney to give you a call."

Me: "Thanks. I appreciate you calling. What can I tell you?"

Detective: "I'm informed you wanted to talk to me about some video you claim to have that has something to do with an unsolved homicide."

Me: "Oh, thanks for calling. But before going on, I'd like to ask you a question."

Detective: "Sure. Go ahead."

Me: "Is this conversation being recorded?"

Detective: "Why? Would that be a problem?"

Me: "Yes. To me, it would. I would prefer to be able to talk freely with you and would not be comfortable doing that if our conversation were being recorded."

Detective: "You haven't done anything wrong, have you?"

Me: "No, I don't think so. Why? Do you think I have?"

Detective: "I hope not. To answer your question, this isn't being recorded. So let's go on. Do you have a video that shows a murder?"

Me: "No, I do not. But I do have a client presently charged with armed robbery who seems to think he does."

Detective: "So you're telling me you don't even know for sure such a video exists."

Me: "Well, can we assume for purposes of this conversation that one does exist? I am pretty sure my client isn't doing this just to piss you off. If my client were to get you such a video, is there anything you and the district attorney would be willing to do to help my client with his current case?"

Detective: "Well, that depends on the video and what it shows. Have you seen it?"

Me: "No."

Detective: "You haven't? Why not?"

Me: "Because for now I don't want to. You better than most must appreciate only too well why I don't want to know for sure what it shows. It could conceivably make me an accessory after the fact to murder, could it not?"

Detective: "Hmmm. You're the lawyer, not me."

Me: "Well, let's just say at this point I don't want people like you accusing me of intentionally withholding evidence of a murder should I admit I actually had such evidence in my possession. For the time being, let's just assume we're discussing a very possible hypothetical, okay? If there is such a tape and it does record a person being shot to death at close range without any apparent justification, would that be of interest to you?"

Detective: "How can I answer that until I know what's on the video?"

Me: "You can tell me, hypothetically speaking, what you and the district attorney would be willing to arrange for my client should he be able to deliver to you such a hypothetical video that hypothetically shows what he is hypothetically claiming it does."

Detective: "Okay, that's very clever. Let me approach this a different way. Can you tell me anything about the victim? Like how about a name?"

Me: "Not at the present time."

Detective: "Why?"

Me: "Frankly, because I haven't asked for a name yet. Like I said, I really don't want to know any more about this yet than I have to. All I can tell you right now is I'm pretty sure it was a male."

Detective: "Pretty sure?"

Me: "No, I'll give you that. I'm really sure the victim was a male."

Detective: "How about the shooter? Male or female?"

Me: "Male."

Detective: "Well, then, we're making some progress. How about telling me *where* this homicide supposedly took place?"

Me: "All I can tell you presently is that I believe it may have happened at a small cabin far out in the desert."

Detective: "Did he give you a description of this cabin or a street or road it's on?"

Me: "No."

Detective: "Do you know when it happened?"

Me: "About a year ago."

Detective: "How does your client know we haven't found the shooter yet?"

Me: "Because he said he knows the shooter and thinks if you knew he had shot my client's friend, you'd have arrested him by now. Which, according to my client, you haven't. He's still out there running around doing his thing —like selling drugs and shooting people."

Detective: "Do you know where the tape is now?"

Me: "No."

Detective: "Since your guy is locked up, do you know who is holding the tape for him?"

Me: "No, I don't know if anybody is. He may have it hidden somewhere. "

Detective: "You've thought this through, huh? Well, without more, I'm not going to be able to tell you anything. You gotta give me more to work on or we're done talking. I'll tell you what. If you give me just a date and location of the homicide, I'll check it out. If anything interesting pops up, I'll talk to the district attorney about a deal for your client. Provided, of course, the video is all your client claims it to be."

Me: "Okay, let me see what I can do."

The next day, I went back to the district attorney to let

him know I'd talked with Morgan and to see if there was anything more I could get from his end by way of a "hypothetical" deal. But I was out of luck there too. His hands were tied, he said, until Detective Morgan gave him the go-ahead, and Morgan was still waiting for some information I was supposed to get for him.

At least that meant the two men had spoken about the issue since I'd spoken with Morgan. Did that show they had more interest in my hypothetical than they were letting me know? Maybe.

The only thing I knew for sure was that on one level I felt like a plump little seal that had found itself swimming with a pack of sharks. Still, on another level it seemed this just might work out better for Darryl than I'd thought at first. Who could know? At the end of the day, the only viable option they'd left me was to get Morgan the minimal information he'd asked for and see if that might loosen their grip on my client's fate.

I got the date and location of the murder from Darryl and passed it on to Morgan. A week went by, then two with no word from either the detective or district attorney. My client's preliminary hearing had already been postponed several times to let Morgan do his thing. And Judge Hewitt was refusing to defer it any further. Surely a body with a name, address, and five bullet holes would have been an event sufficiently noteworthy to make Morgan's department take some notice. Unless somebody—like the man in the yellow house—had managed to dispose of the body before anyone else stumbled over it and reported it to the authorities.

Even so, I should have heard something back from the detective or district attorney. The math wasn't that complicated. Either they had no record of such a homicide, or they did and hadn't yet found the perpetrator. Either way, they should have wanted to see Darryl's tape. So what was their holdup?

As it turned out, it wasn't until the morning of my client's preliminary hearing that I finally got anything from either of them. When I stopped by my office to pick up Darryl's file before going to court, I found a message from Detective Morgan on the answering machine, asking me to give him a call. I called back but without success. Maybe Morgan was already at court. Or the district attorney might have some information. With some hope for good news, I hurried to the courthouse.

When I walked in from the parking lot, I was a little taken back when I noticed the district attorney with Detective Morgan beside him coming toward me across the courtyard. The look on their faces set off alarms in my mind. Something was clearly up.

When we got close enough, I opened the ball. "Hey gentlemen, what's up?"

"Well, I checked out the information you gave me," Detective Morgan said.

"And—?"

"And I'm sorry, but we aren't interested."

Shocked, I asked, "What does that mean?"

"It means my department has no interest in pursuing your client's supposed video."

A cocky smile some might have called a smirk added to

the information I'd just been given. Trouble was, I wasn't sure what to make of it or how to respond. So I didn't.

Simply put, I was stunned and also a bit confused. Something about all this was definitely not right, but I didn't want either of them to know it. So I just looked at the two men with as good a poker face as I could muster and said nothing.

One thing I was sure of was that Darryl wouldn't be bluffing empty-handed with men who held his future in their hands. I had no doubt Darryl had witnessed a murder. I had no doubt he'd videotaped that murder. Moreover, I had no doubt the murderer was still roaming free.

What I did have doubts about was why a homicide detective would not be interested in a murder my client was more than willing to help him solve. Unless the shooter was connected with someone powerful enough to be calling the shots.

Adding to the odor of the stink I was starting to smell was why Morgan had come to court just to tell me he didn't care to see the video. Wouldn't a phone call have sufficed? Couldn't the district attorney have delivered that message?

In short, why was Morgan here in the courtyard this morning with the district attorney? If no deal were to be made, they didn't need to tell me that in person. So were they here together to discuss something other than turning down my client's offer? Logic and reason suggested there had to be some reason they weren't sharing with me.

So what would that reason be? Did it have anything to

do with me? I couldn't say it did. But then again, I couldn't rule it out either.

At last, I simply said, "Okay."

A pause ensued before the district attorney spoke up to fill in the conversational void. "So how can you be sure your client really has the video showing a murder he told you about?"

Given Morgan's just-expressed disinterest in the video, this was an awkward question. Like some kind of trick question you might expect from a district attorney if you were being cross-examined in court. In a state of mild alarm, I asked myself, *Are they hoping for Morgan to witness an admission on my part as to the existence of a video that he could later testify about in court? Surely not!*

I couldn't be sure they weren't trying to set me up for something I could only guess at. So in an abundance of caution, I responded with a smile, "What video?"

They quickly glanced at each other, then back at me before the district attorney reflexively blurted out, "What?"

Without losing my smile, I again responded, "What video are you talking about?"

At that, a Mona Lisa smile formed on the district attorney's face while the one on Morgan's face dissolved. Apparently done with whatever he'd come to court for, the detective finally said, "Well, I guess that's that. See you guys around."

As he walked away, some of the harsh realities of possible machinations from an alternative universe that resided somewhere outside the orbit of the law started bouncing around in my mind. As the district attorney and I walked toward the court, he said, "Well, I'm sorry that didn't work out for your client. But just to show how much we appreciate your trying to do the right thing, I've got an offer for your client I don't think he can refuse."

"Really?" I asked, still on high alert. "What is that?"

"If he pleads today, I'm willing to give him low term on one count of commercial burglary. That's only a sixteen-month sentence. With good-time/half-time, he should be out in only a little over eight months. That will also allow him to plead to a felony that isn't a strike under California's three strikes law, unlike robbery with a gun, which *is* one. Pretty good, huh? Just know that this offer expires at the commencement of the preliminary hearing this morning. He either accepts the offer this morning or he takes his chances at trial."

Pretty good?

I was astonished!

Given that they had security video and two live witnesses to Darryl's armed robbery, it was *too* good.

Again, I was left wondering why. Just a few weeks earlier, the district attorney had offered my client ten years in state prison if he would plead to a felony that would have counted as a strike. Now he was offering only sixteen months for a plea to a non-strike offense? Why?

Then it hit me with a jolt.

Could it be that Mr. Big really was *that* big? That the tentacles of his power and influence, to which Darryl had attested, reached so far as to influence even some who operated within the hallowed halls of our legal system—like the district attorney? Or Morgan? Or both?

If that were true, Mr. Big's reach would no doubt extend even more efficiently to those who walked the dangerous hallways of our county's jails and state prisons. I couldn't help but wonder. Was Darryl being offered a deal he couldn't resist, not knowing that in fact he'd already been given a death sentence by the man who lived in the big yellow house by the highway?

Maybe—or maybe not. But sometimes things that seem too good to be true can often turn out to be bad. *Really* bad!

And like Papa used to tell me, sometimes if a man thinks he's smarter than he really is, he very well might find himself one day digging his own grave.

Is that what Darryl did?

I'll never know. After Darryl took the plea deal, I never saw or heard from him again.

Little did I know at the time that I too would soon be offered something too good to be true and that it would lead me to encounter yet another variety of evil.

He has dug a pit and hollowed it out,
and has fallen into the hole, which he made.
His mischief will return upon his own head.[2]

You shall not distort justice; you shall not be partial.... Justice, and only justice you shall pursue that you may live.[1]

～

20

HOW INJUSTICE IS SERVED

Judges are human. They all make mistakes. Some have bad tempers. Others are rude. A few are prejudiced. More than a few are narcissists. A few are even criminal.

Rarely, however, does an attorney encounter a judge with all these traits.

When it does happen, it can leave the attorney emotionally traumatized by an experience best described by just one word—evil.

Judge G. Erpman was such a man.

Physically, ethically, and morally, Erpman was a small man who combed his close-cropped wavy gray hair forward in the style of a Caesar. Lacking only a laurel wreath to complete the image, he ruled over those who came into his court with the contempt and iron fist of Nero himself.

Like many judges, he was a former district attorney. Unlike most, he clearly presumed the guilt of most criminal defendants brought before him. The presumption of a defendant's innocence until their guilt could be proven beyond a reasonable doubt was a concept Judge Erpman had left somewhere in the past of his earlier life for lesser mortals to fiddle with.

To obtain yet mask his goal of achieving a conviction in most cases brought before him, Erpman was a master at the art of plausible deniability. This skill allowed him to insert subtle statements, smirks, a tilting of his head, or an almost undetectable rolling of the eyes that conveyed his contempt for his intended victims—my client in this case— as well as their counsel—i.e., attorneys like me who stooped to defend those he considered vermin. But these gestures were made with just enough reserve and finesse he could not be directly accused of anything prejudicial.

Meanwhile, he denied or overruled the motions and objections of any defendant's counsel while granting almost all those offered by the prosecution. It didn't take long for any defense attorney in his court to gain a sense that the field upon which they were playing was not level. Unfortunately, Erpman was clever enough to make the degree of uphill slant he imposed upon any defense attorney appearing before him nearly impossible to prove. It was like suffering death by bleeding from a thousand small cuts.

The only thing you could know for sure at the end of a trial in Erpman's court was you'd most assuredly been "Erp'd on"—a term coined by those defense attorneys who regularly had matters assigned to his court. For attorneys who survived this emotionally and psychologically brutal experience, the only remaining hope was the appellate court's post-trial review of Erpman's rulings, which automatically followed the conviction and sentencing of defendants.

Defense attorneys left Erpman's court thinking, *Thank God for the court record!* This was the trial transcript that would be forwarded by the court reporter to the court of appeals after any felony trial ending in a conviction. A possible reversal at least offered defendants the hope of a new trial in front of a judge other than Erpman. But to get there, attorneys and their clients had to endure the torture of the Erpman experience.

In my first appearance in his court, when I stated my name, Cliff Nichols, for the record, Erpman asked me with a condescending smirk, "Do you spell your last name with one or two 'g's, counselor?" That set the contemptuous tone for almost everything that came out his mouth in my following appearances before him.

A month or so before, Judge Hewitt's clerk had called me in to take on an attempted murder case involving an individual named Alejandro. At the time it was offered to me, it seemed too good to be true. Attempted murder cases were often reserved for the better, more experienced criminal defense attorneys. So when I was asked to take the case, I felt flattered and took it as a promotion.

Soon afterward, however, at the preliminary hearing with Judge Hewitt, Alejandro's case was advanced to Superior Court for trial. Until then, I had no way of knowing that Hewitt would be assigning it to none other than the court of Judge Erpman. All that to say, had I known

Erpman would be the judge assigned to Alejandro's trial for attempted murder when Hewitt's clerk first called me to take the case, I probably would have been far better off to have declined to take the case at all. Unfortunately, by then it was too late.

So much for the promotion. I was soon to learn that it really had been too good to be true.

The case involving Alejandro all started on a Sunday evening several months earlier with the shooting of a man named Jim in a deserted parking lot on the far side of town. Dusk was just creeping in, and the automatic parking lot lights hadn't yet switched on. That is, except for one light directly above an ATM from which Jim was trying to coax the money he needed. Why he needed the cash, he couldn't remember later, but the machine just wasn't giving it to him.

As he tried a second time to get the machine to accept his debit card, he failed to notice a man coming up behind him. That is, until the man spoke up in a snarly voice, "Hurry up, %#&!."

Without thought, Jim responded under his breath with a reciprocal expletive as he continued trying to get the machine to work.

Apparently, the other man had heard Jim's muttering and rejoined with, "%#&! me? You're the one who's going to be %#&! if you don't hurry up, you %#&."

Annoyed now by the stranger's belligerence, Jim reflexively turned to respond with yet another expletive. He saw the gun just before a .22 caliber bullet passed through his upper left arm, coming to rest in his left lung just an inch to the left of his heart. Jim crumpled down to the ground. He said nothing more to the man—or to anyone else for that matter until he eventually was able to speak to the sheriff's deputies who accompanied him to the hospital.

All he could remember was that the shooter was a short guy with dark hair straddling a small bicycle. The man might have been Hispanic, but he couldn't be sure as the shadowy dusk offered no illumination beyond the glow of the ATM light. The one thing he could be sure of was that the guy on the bike had a handgun pointed right at him and that in the twinkling of an eye a blast had spewed from the gun barrel.

ATM records revealed that Jim never did get the cash he was after. Which was a good thing as everyone involved in the case agreed it would likely have ended up in the pocket of the guy on the bike.

Other than Jim, the only witness willing to cooperate with the officers who arrived at the scene was an elderly woman who didn't speak English very well. Through an interpreter, it was determined she'd been standing across the parking lot about fifty feet from the ATM when she heard the shot. With a look over to where the noise had come from, she'd seen a male riding a small bike away from Jim's body. She hadn't been close enough to see the shooter's face or whether the man was Hispanic or white, but she was pretty sure he wasn't black.

Beyond that, she could state only that the man on the bike had headed north. The first responders immediately put out a broadcast with the following details: "Shots fired. Civilian wounded. Suspect is a male with dark hair riding a small bike. Last seen heading north from the given location of the ATM. Suspect is armed and dangerous. Caution advised."

After hearing the broadcast, one officer patrolling several blocks to the *west* of the ATM stopped a young male Hispanic riding a small bike. After questioning and photographing the young man, he let the possible suspect go without bothering to take down the young man's name, address, or any telephone number by which he could later be contacted.

When asked about this, the officer only said, "I searched him for a weapon and didn't find one. So I let him go. We weren't going to arrest every kid who just happened to be on a bike that night."

No other possible suspects were found that night, much less stopped or questioned by any sheriff deputies in connection with the shooting.

Enter Alejandro.

Alejandro was a nineteen-year-old active gang-banger. His gang-related operations were all conducted out of his parents' home where he lived. Unfortunately for Alejandro, their house was just north of the ATM where Jim was shot. Like many of his gang compatriots, he was short, had black hair, and was known to the gang detail of the local division of the sheriff's department.

Perhaps more unfortunate for Alejandro was that this had all occurred only a few blocks from the home where a gang detail detective named Janson was raising his family. Shooting or no shooting, he'd long before let it be known that he did not like Alejandro being in his neighborhood.

Janson also happened to be the detective assigned to investigate the attempted murder of Jim.

A few days after the shooting, Janson visited Jim in the hospital to show him a photo six-pack—i.e., photos of six young males with black hair affixed to a cardboard—to see if Jim could identify any of them as the shooter. Was it mere coincidence that Janson happened to include the young Hispanic gang-banger he wanted out of his neighborhood in the photo lineup?

In any case, Jim's testimony in the initial interview was that Alejandro's face looked closest to what he remembered of the shooter, *but he couldn't be sure it was him.* At least that's what Janson put in his report. But for all practical purposes, Janson chose to interpret Jim's uncertainty as a positive identification that Alejandro was the shooter.

Early the next morning, the sheriff deputies raided the home of Alejandro's parents and took Alejandro into custody. Booked for attempted murder, Alejandro claimed to know nothing about the events that could now put him in prison for life. He insisted that Janson had been out to get him for a long time due to his association with the La Raza street gang that operated in Janson's neighborhood. Framing Alejandro for this shooting was just the next step in an already bad relationship between Janson and Alejandro.

According to Alejandro, Janson had once beat him to a pulp, then arrested him on bogus charges that were later dismissed for lack of evidence. On another, the detective had driven Alejandro several miles out into the desert after dark, where he'd confiscated Alejandro's shoes, leaving him to walk home barefoot. These were just some of the notable encounters he claimed to have had with this detective.

Based on Alejandro's story, I filed a motion for discovery of all disciplinary actions the sheriff's department might have on record against Janson as well as any arrests or detainments of my client that in any way involved Janson. To support the motion, I attached my client's affidavit attesting to Janson's pattern of harassment.

This quickly got sticky for a couple of reasons. First, Janson took the contents of the affidavit as a personal accusation by me—not Alejandro—that he had engaged in criminal conduct. Secondly, Janson and his wife happened to be members of the same church my family and I attended.

The Sunday following my filing of the motion, Janson confronted me in the church lobby in front of both our wives. Before I knew what was happening, he made the case that by filing my motion I was guilty of making false accusations against a brother in Christ. The tone of his lowered voice and his redness of face could best be described as controlled fury.

After he finished, I did my own best to calmly explain that the accusations were my client's, not mine. They were also an integral part of my client's defense—that Janson was railroading him—to which he was entitled by law. My job was to investigate the claims and present that defense to the best of my abilities.

At the time, the explanation seemed to calm Janson, who said no more. I assumed the issue was now resolved and went on into church giving it little further thought. At least until much later.

I rather suspected my client was telling the truth about Janson. Clearly, the detective didn't like Alejandro, and Alejandro certainly didn't like him. Even Janson was willing to admit that. But there were little things I discovered that corroborated Alejandro's claims of bias beyond Janson's newly-developed dislike for me.

For instance, Alejandro's court-appointed investigator learned that when Jim had been shown the photo six-pack in the hospital, Janson's index finger kept tapping only on Alejandro's photo the entire time Jim was looking at them. Nor did Janson ever present to Jim in any photo six-pack the photo taken by the officer of the only young man riding a bike that night near the scene of the crime. A young man who bore a strong resemblance to Alejandro. Why? Was Janson afraid Jim might have identified the kid on the bike as the shooter? Was this something Janson didn't want to risk because of his desire to have Alejandro take the fall for the crime?

If having a detective like Janson in his life wasn't bad enough, Alejandro had no way of foreseeing that his journey with Janson would soon cross paths with Judge Erpman, from which point things would only get worse.

True to form, Erpman summarily denied my motion seeking evidence that might corroborate Janson's bias toward Alejandro. For him, any evidence of Janson's bias was of concern only to an overwrought defense counsel and could be obtained informally out of court from the district attorney if any existed. Yeah, right! Something as likely as my going to Mars! More likely, Erpman believed the detective's bias to be entirely justified since Alejandro was a known gang member, therefore by definition scum that deserved only scorn and inevitable incarceration.

This precedent set the tone for the ensuing trial. Erpman wasn't interested in having the jury hear details of how Janson might have been harassing Alejandro for several years before the shooting nor even that they resided in the same neighborhood. To Erpman such testimony was *not relevant*.

Also deemed irrelevant was the fact that Alejandro looked very much like the young man whose photo had never been shown to Jim. Erpman excluded that photo's introduction into evidence and expressly barred any reference to it during cross-examination of witnesses or in my closing argument. As a consequence, the jury was never even informed of the existence of that young mystery man, much less ever allowed to see his photo and compare his resemblance to Alejandro.

These were just some of the ways Erpman came to the aid of the prosecution. And if ever there was a case where such help was needed to gain a conviction, this might well have been one. The ATM security camera had failed to capture any image of the shooter, his weapon, or his bike. No .22 caliber handgun was ever recovered from Alejandro, his parents, or anywhere else for that matter, much less ever entered into evidence at trial.

In fact, the only weapon found during the raid of Alejandro's parents' house was a .22 rifle stored in a closet in the parents' bedroom. Alejandro's father told Janson it had only been used a few times for hunting jackrabbits. That alone didn't aid the prosecution's case. But the closet also contained a small box of .22 caliber shells from which two bullets were missing.

Judge Erpman did allow the prosecutor to admit that box of shells into evidence to show the jury that Alejandro had access to bullets of the same caliber used on Jim. All my objections that this evidence was irrelevant, lacking foundation, and extremely prejudicial to the defendant were overruled. According to Erpman, the two missing shells supported the district attorney's supposedly legitimate *inference* that one of the rounds could have been used by Alejandro on Jim at the ATM. By that logic, *any* box of ammunition missing a bullet in Alejandro's neighborhood could be introduced into evidence for the same purpose. Ridiculous? Not to Erpman.

Nor was any small bike ever recovered in Alejandro's possession or at his parents' home. The only thing remotely close to one was the bare frame of a bike Janson recovered from a heap of broken furniture and other discarded trash in the parents' backyard. It had no tires, chain, handlebars, or even peddles. Nor were any such items ever recovered from the heap where the frame had been retrieved.

Yet again, Erpman rose to the occasion to rescue the prosecutor. Over my objections, he allowed the frame to be placed into evidence to support the *inference* it could have been used in the shooting based on speculation by Detective Janson that Alejandro could have dismantled the bike and discarded the parts to hide evidence of the crime.

"Objection, pure speculation, Your Honor. Lacking foundation and highly prejudicial, Your Honor."

"Overruled."

Why Alejandro would get rid of the handlebars, peddles and tires but not the frame of the bike made no sense—except to the prosecution and Erpman. And so went his trial. Smirks of annoyance crossing Erpman's face conveyed to the jury his contempt for any attorney who dared raise objections he considered specious. Similarly, he denied my defense motions with patronizing tilts of his head. Meanwhile, highly questionable evidence and testimony offered by the prosecution was admitted with a fleeting smile and subtle nods conveying approval to the jury.

This included Jim's own testimony. In the months he'd been visiting with Detective Janson, his identification of the shooter had gone from his original "it could be Alejandro, but I'm not sure" to breaking into tears during the trial while pointing at Alejandro from across the court.

"I'm sorry to have taken up so much of your time," he told the jury, "but I have no doubt the man who shot me is that man seated right over there."

That was the moment I figured had swung the trial in Janson's favor. But before the jury could hang its hat on Jim's testimony to convict Alejandro for a crime he may not have committed, Erpman took the opportunity to deliver the coup de grace.

Right in the middle of my closing argument on Alejandro's behalf, Erpman interrupted with a look on his face that suggested he could no longer bear the boredom and so presumed the jury also needed a break. He called for a one-hour recess and informed all in the court that the argument that would decide the fate of the remainder of this nineteen-year-old's entire life could resume after the break. Inferred by Erpman's facial expression were two final words that remained unstated—*if necessary.*

By the time the trial ended, I felt like I'd been put through the tumbling under-tow of a crashing tidal wave, desperately fighting for breath and unable to determine which way was up. The jury did convict Alejandro, after which Judge Erpman sentenced him to serve from thirteen years to life in state prison for the crime of attempted murder.

Some months later, the Court of Appeals notified me that, based on its review of the trial transcript, Alejandro's conviction had been upheld. I was left shocked and saddened. Surely the conviction could have been reversed based on several of Erpman's evidentiary rulings alone.

But it wasn't. For my part, there was nothing left to be done. Erpman had won.

What I had no way of knowing was that the case involving Alejandro was still far from being over. At least as far as I was concerned. In fact, it could be fairly concluded that what was yet to come would prove far worse.

Justice is turned back, and righteousness stands far away; for truth has stumbled in the street.[2] *They devise injustices, saying, "We are ready with a well-conceived plot."*[3]

*All this I have seen and applied to my mind ... a man [who] has
exercised authority over another man to his hurt. So then, I have [also]
seen the wicked buried, ... and they are soon forgotten in the city
where they did thus. This too is futility.*[1]

21

A RECORD BROKEN

About a month after Erpman sentenced Alejandro to
prison, I received a call from one of the elders of
my church. He wanted to know if he could come to my
house for a visit.

"Of course," I said. "But tell me, what's up? Is there
anything in particular you want to talk about?"

I thought maybe he wanted to nominate me to some
position of church leadership. Boy, was I wrong!

"If you don't mind," the elder responded, "I'm going
to be bringing Detective Janson with me. We both have an
issue we need to talk to you about regarding the trial you
both just finished."

Surprised, all I could think to say was, "Sure. Come
on by."

We set a time for them to stop by that afternoon. I'd
arranged for my wife to take the kids to the park and

turned on my favorite mood music—Mozart's *Requiem*. I was pretty sure of what these guys wanted to talk about and figured a certain solemnity would help set the tone.

Sure enough, there was awkwardness from the moment the two men stepped inside my house. Out the gate and for no reason I could think of other than pure intimidation, Janson slowly pulled his semi-automatic pistol from his jacket pocket and laid it beside himself on the sofa.

"You don't mind my bringing this in, I hope. I didn't want to leave it in the car but also didn't want you not to know I had it with me."

I looked from Janson to the elder before saying, "No problem. Make yourself at home." But I was thinking, *What kind of jerk brings a gun to a meeting with a church elder?*

In contrast to Janson, the elder laid his Bible on the coffee table and cleared his throat before taking up the issue Janson had raised in the church lobby several months before. Namely, his being wrongfully accused of a crime by a brother in Christ.

"I thought we'd resolved that!" I cut in lamely.

"No, it hasn't been resolved," Janson said.

"You accused me of crimes. As a brother, I think it necessary to take this to the next level."

"The next level?"

The elder opened his Bible, "Yes. We're here in accordance with Matthew 18." He read aloud:

> *If your brother sins, go and show him*
> *his fault in private; if he listens to*
> *you, you have won your brother. But*

*if he does not listen to you, take one or
two more with you, so that by the
mouth of two or three witnesses every
fact may be confirmed. If he refuses to
listen to them, tell it to the church;
and if he refuses to listen even to the
church, let him be to you as a Gentile
and a tax collector .[2]*

In other words, they were here to talk about possibly kicking my butt out of church!?! Well, that was certainly something new—for me at least.

I stared at the two men, astonished. "So, based on that, I'm guessing this get-together would be level two. Correct?"

"Yes," the elder responded solemnly. Janson had a smug look on his face as though assured he would prevail.

The following conversation devolved into my prior discussion with Janson about it being my duty to defend my client. In any case, my client's allegations had all been effectively rendered moot by Erpman. In a sense, Janson had been vindicated by Alejandro's conviction. Or, so I argued. But apparently that was not enough for Janson. He wanted me to admit my *sin* in front of the elder and failing that before the entire church.

"So what exactly are you looking for me to say?" I asked.

"That you were wrong when you allowed Alejandro's lies about me to be placed in the public record," Janson quickly interjected. "And I want you to admit that by doing it you committed a sin against me."

"Or what?" I asked, even more astonished.

"Then we'll take it to level three in accordance with Scripture and go before the church with the issue," Janson demanded.

Unfortunately for Janson, somewhere in this conversation he'd lost the certainty—and thus support—of the elder sitting next to him. The doubt on the man's face indicated he was becoming less and less sure that what I had done to defend my client was a *sin* versus any attorney's professional obligation.

I turned to the elder and asked, "So what are you proposing? That I admit to you something I'm not convinced I did or I'm going to be brought before the whole church so they can kick out not only me but my entire family for doing nothing more than my duty to defend my client? If that's the case, I think you're making a big mistake. But do what you think you have to do."

With that and the help I'm pretty sure Mozart was bringing to the fray, Janson soon found himself in a stalemate. Ultimately, the elder rendered his decision that level three would be neither necessary nor appropriate. Janson and I should agree to disagree, resolve the matter with a handshake, and move on.

To close the issue, I turned to the detective. "Look, Janson. If Alejandro's allegations put you in a bad light, I'm sorry that had to happen. But you can take it to the bank the jury gave little credence to Alejandro's version, as proven by his conviction. And if you feel you need more, you can always tell people everything I put out there was disproved as evidenced by the fact that I lost the trial."

Janson picked up his gun from my sofa and slid it back into his shoulder holster. I could tell he was even angrier than when he'd first walked into my living room. Still, if he shot me now, he'd also have to shoot the elder. Defaulting to a far preferable Plan B, we all stood and frigidly shook hands. The two men then left, mumbling something about thanks for your time and isn't God good.

Thank God.

For me, the incident only gave greater veracity to Alejandro's version of Janson's character. As they drove away, I felt what Alejandro must have felt when he found himself in Janson's crosshairs, which is where I was fairly sure I remained in Janson's view at the end of our meeting. It was not a good feeling.

Unfortunately, it was not nearly as bad a feeling as another kick in the gut still coming my way in connection with this case. About two years after Alejandro's trial, I was walking across the pavilion of another courthouse on the other side of the county when I noticed a woman I vaguely recognized. It took me a moment to remember where I'd seen her before. Then it came to me. She was the court reporter for Judge Erpman in Alejandro's trial.

The woman waved to me with recognition as though she wanted to talk. I approached her, and we exchanged the cordial greeting of two basic strangers who have only one shared experience giving them any reason to speak— in our case, Erpman.

With suppressed sarcasm, I asked her how the judge

was doing. Immediately, her expression grew serious and even troubled. "I don't know and I don't care. Though I've been hoping I might run into you one day so I could talk to you about the trial you did in his court."

"Really?" I said. "After that trial, I'd have thought you wouldn't want to see me ever again. That was painful."

Her expression grew even more troubled. "It *was* painful. That's why I've wanted to talk to you for the longest time. I haven't because I've also been afraid to. "

"Afraid? Why?"

"I wanted to apologize for being a part of all that went down in that trial. Not long after it ended, I decided I couldn't take Erpman anymore and put in for a transfer out of his court. When he found out, he got furious and threatened to ruin me. But my mind was made up. I wasn't going to be threatened by him anymore and forced to play his games. The man was evil. And I wanted no part of him anymore."

I jumped in, "What do you mean by *his games?*"

"Well, something I'm pretty sure you don't know," she said, averting her eyes. "He played with the record."

"What do you mean he *played with the record?*"

She lowered her voice. "Look, I'm going to tell you. But if anybody ever asks me, I'll deny knowing anything about it. Understood?"

"Sure. Understood. Now what are you talking about?"

"Judge Erpman knew some of the things he did were questionable, and he didn't want them to appear in the court transcript. So he had a signal he demanded I follow."

"What do you mean?" I asked.

Dropping her voice even lower, she disclosed, "When I started working with him, he ordered me to follow certain hand signals. In the beginning, it didn't seem like a bad thing. And you have to understand I didn't think I had any choice. You know the system. If one judge fires you or lets it be known you're trouble, other judges shy away from you. I'm raising two boys on my own, so I couldn't afford that. But I put in for jobs in other courts beyond Erpman's reach. And the minute I got one, I was out of there."

"I still don't understand. What signal are you talking about?"

Her face grew red as she explained with obvious embarrassment mixed with even more apparent shame, "When a defense attorney made objections or motions Erpman knew were valid but that he didn't want in the record, he would put his hand on the front edge of his bench with his fingers over the edge. The standing order was that if he raised his fingers UP to point straight out, he wanted to be off the record and I was to stop typing. When he dropped his fingers DOWN again, we were back on the record, and I was to resume typing."

I felt like the wind had been kicked out of me. "Do you mean what I think you're saying?"

"Yes. That's what I'm apologizing for. A lot, if not most, of your better objections and motions he didn't want any appellate court to see—and even some of his responsive rulings—did NOT make the record."

Still trying to absorb the enormity of what she'd just revealed, I asked the obvious, "He *knew* what he was doing was wrong and didn't want the Court of Appeals to get a complete transcript that should have memorialized it?"

"Exactly."

"That's beyond criminal! That's evil."

"That's why I quit. I had to change courthouses because I was sure he'd come after me. And I didn't want to have to guess how. Honestly, I was scared. He's scary. It's also why I felt for so long I needed to talk to you. But until I saw you today, I was afraid of doing even that. I hope you can forgive me, but at least now it's off my chest. I just hope in some ways it makes you feel a little better about your trial."

"But what about the defendant?"

"That's on Erpman. I repeat, if you ever tell anybody what I just told you, I'll deny it. Look, I'm telling you this now to get it off my chest. But I don't even want to think what Erpman might do if he knew I'd talked to you about this. Like I said, he's evil."

That last part I already knew!

The import of what she'd told me was based on the fact that after a conviction like Alejandro's, the defense attorney files for an appeal with the appellate court, then moves on with his own life. The trial transcript is then directed by the trial court to the appellate court, where it gets passed on to the appellate attorneys. In the entire process, the original defense attorney is very unlikely to ever—read, *almost never*—have any reason to even see, much less read, that transcript. So if the appellate attorneys received a "cleansed" or "doctored" transcript, a defense attorney like me would likely never be made aware of it.

As Erpman knew!

In short, if what the court reporter had just told me were true, many of the grounds for Alejandro's conviction to be overturned on appeal might never have been considered because the various objections I'd made didn't even exist in the transcript the appellate attorneys would have reviewed. Even if I'd discovered this earlier, I'd have no way of recollecting all the objections I'd raised, much less the grounds I'd given Erpman to support them. Even worse, there was no way to ever prove Erpman's pre-arranged slight-of-hand had ever happened.

I walked away from that exchange with my thoughts raging like the lightning and fierce wind of a category five hurricane. What kind of dark soul could do what Erpman had done? What evil from a man whose job it was to mete out justice? Erpman had not only broken the record, but also—in my book—had broken some kind of record for doing something that was purely evil.

For some reason, it brought to mind another unforgettable exchange I'd had thirteen years ago now with a woman named Savannah Georgia Booth. I couldn't stop thinking about what she'd done her best to impress upon me back then.

For our struggle is not against flesh
and blood, but against the rulers,
against the powers, against the world
forces of this darkness, against the

spiritual forces of wickedness in the
heavenly places. Therefore, take up the
full armor of God, so that you will be
able to resist in the evil day, and
having done everything, to stand
firm. [3]

In the years since my conversation with Ms. Booth, I'd resumed going to church every Sunday, read my Bible, and attended more weekly Bible Studies than I could count. But to what end? Had any of it sunk in? What difference to my life and those around me had all of this really made?

Not much, apparently, based on the bombshell the court reporter had just dropped on me. In my dealings with Erpman, I'd completely overlooked the spiritual dimension of the battle Ms. Booth had told me about so long ago in the context of Alejandro's trial. The court reporter's words now drove this home to me like a spear through my heart. Contemplating the evil that was Erpman caused my mind to turn toward the shallowness of my own spiritual life, which seemed to have gained so little ground despite my increased attention to the "religion" of attending church and Bible studies.

In the movie *The Godfather, Part III*, Michael Corleone makes this same point to a priest toward the end of his life. The priest is assuring him that he has spent a life involved with the church and done many good deeds as a result, so he didn't need to worry about the fate of his soul. Michael responds by retrieving a good-sized rock from a nearby stream. He broke the wet rock in two and showed the priest that though this rock had been submerged in water for decades, if not centuries, on the inside it was still completely dry. The point Michael Corleone was making is that in a spiritual sense that rock was him.

Was that rock also me? I'd spent years immersed in a life that was all about the spiritual. But little had penetrated to my inner core to transform the way I lived and thought. During Alejandro's trial, my efforts to petition the God I professed as my Lord to assist me, guide me, and direct me in that battle were non-existent, for all practical purposes. On the inside I remained as dry as that rock.

In short, after my talk with Erpman's former court reporter, I was convicted that I was a "religious" man who was living life as a practical atheist. In one sense, I could be standing among the accused when the writer of the letter to the Hebrews said:

> *You have become dull of hearing. For though by this time you ought to be teachers, you have need again for someone to teach you the elementary principles of the oracles of God, and you have come to need milk and not solid food. For everyone who partakes only of milk is not accustomed to the word of righteousness, for he is an infant. But solid food is for the mature, who because of practice have their senses trained to discern good and evil.* [4]

Then again, by God's grace maybe my experience with Erpman was helping me to grow and turn a corner toward a greater spiritual maturity. All I knew in the days, weeks, months, and years following my conversation with Erpman's court reporter was that it took the evil of a man like Erpman to make me appreciate my previous short-comings as an effective champion for good in the face of evil.

My conclusion? For evil to exist, there must also exist that which is good by comparison. And if that which is good is universal, what can its source be than a God from whom all good things must flow?

In part, maybe that was God's purpose for allowing my life's journey to cross paths with the likes of Butch and Sundance, E. Blotnick, Brock M., Detective Morgan, and now Judge Erpman.

Going forward, one thing I knew clearly. The more people like Erpman imposed their evil to darken my world, the more I needed God to bring his goodness and light to these situations. In short, to deal with what is evil in this world, I needed God's help more than I'd realized.

God implores us to petition him for his protection, guidance, and wisdom when dealing with such evil. From that day forward, I resolved to be a man who would no longer let men like Erpman be used by spiritual forces of darkness to rain injury upon those around him without my acting upon that belief. In other words, I resolved to live as though I actually believed that God *is real and a rewarder to those who seek him.*[5] And so I prayed that God would give me the strength to carry out this new resolve.

Sadly, given the plausible deniability of all the court reporter had revealed, there was little to be done for Alejandro. Any investigation of Erpman would have necessitated getting the court reporter to repeat to someone— like me wearing a wire—recording her admission as to what she'd participated in. In any case, betraying this mother of two's trust in me and opening her up to criminal prosecution to *maybe* get Alejandro a new trial was a choice I didn't even think to make back then.

All I could think of in the moment was that God loves justice and will not forsake his godly ones.[6] So as I walked away from the court reporter, that was the substance of my prayer: *Lord, let there be justice in the case of Erpman to address the injustice of Alejandro's trial.*

It wasn't much later that I learned that Judge Erpman was being investigated for sexually molesting his own twelve-year-old daughter. Was that an answer to my prayer? So long as I remain in the land of the living, I'll never know. If it were, it certainly took a form I could never have anticipated.

Either way, perhaps it should have been proof to me that Papa had been right on yet another subject. If this investigation of Erpman was of God, he sure proved himself capable of coming up with circumstances to achieve his purpose in a way I would never have foreseen. Kind of like a helicopter full of deputies arriving on a mountaintop to deal with Butch and Sundance. A college professor letting me sit with him until the police cleared a building I shouldn't have been in. A cab driver doing a U-turn to save me from two gang-bangers. And a secretary risking her job to suggest I visit her friend to learn more about Jesus.

In Erpman's case, because he was a sitting Superior Court judge, the detective in charge of the child molestation investigation involving him called him one morning to let him know he was to be arrested later that day. This was a courtesy they were allowing so he could make whatever arrangements he thought necessary before being taken into custody.

As it turned out, one of the *arrangements* Erpman considered imperative was to avoid at all costs being incarcerated with inmates he'd treated so contemptuously in the course of his career. The next day, the papers reported that Erpman had died from a self-inflicted gunshot to the head.

Fittingly, one article about his suicide carried a quote from an attorney that would have made an apt epitaph on Erpman's tombstone: "Appearing in court before Erpman was the worst experience in my professional life."

An understatement, considering Erpman was a man who gave new meaning to a record being broken.

What I had no way of knowing at the time was how God had used Erpman to bring me to a place in my spiritual walk where I would need to be to handle what was coming next.

Do not be deceived, God is not mocked; for whatever a man sows, this he will also reap.[7]

Everyone must be quick to hear, slow to speak and slow to anger.[1] *For anger slays the foolish man.*[2]

$$\sim$$

22

HARD KNOCKS ARE SOMETIMES GOOD

It was early afternoon. Court was once again in recess and so I decided to take a break from doing very little.

I had been waiting for my case to be called by Judge Hewitt since 8:30 that morning. But due to the court's heavy calendar—or so Hewitt's clerk said—it had yet to be called.

That was life in court. As I'd learned from Cummings several years before, you could be kept waiting forever, but you'd better not be late. Thus the litigator's mantra: *hurry up and wait.* Something especially true in Hewitt's court. Courtesy to attorneys and their schedules was not his strong suit.

I didn't dare go far. Heaven help me if my case were called and I couldn't be found. Hewitt would just trail it to the next day, thus returning the whole process back to the beginning. But to get a brief change of scenery, I stepped outside the front door of the courthouse.

I was immediately reminded that this was a hot August

afternoon, well over 110 degrees in the sun. Being a prudent man, I leaned against a nearby wall to take advantage of the 95-degree shade it provided. Meanwhile, I apathetically took note of a few other people meandering around the courtyard from one source of shade to another while they too waited for their cases to be called. I must confess my mind was elsewhere.

A few weeks earlier, a letter had arrived in our home mailbox from the district attorney's office. It was a notice to my now ex-wife, informing her she'd been charged with floating several bad checks and was ordered to answer the charges on a certain date in none other than Judge Hewitt's court. The same court from which came many of my cases that brought us an income!

In ensuing conversations, I'd discovered she'd also maxed out numerous credit cards due to a series of large cash withdrawals. But that wasn't the worst of it. Among other things, she never would confess—to me, at any rate —where all the money had gone. I had my reasons to believe I knew, but now isn't the time to go into all that.

What's important here are two things. First, this experience is what cracked the shell of trust I'd thought we had in our marriage, which would eventually lead to its shattering several years later and our going our separate ways. More importantly, it also provided my life with another spiritual pivot point that I would take with me long after the marriage ended.

At the beginning of this episode, my wife flew back to her parent's ranch for a few days to seek the comfort of her mother, leaving our sons and the debt she'd incurred for me to deal with. More specifically, she wanted the reassurances of her mother, with whom she'd had telephone contact almost every day or at the least every week since we were married.

At first, I'd thought these frequent calls were helpful to get my wife past her homesickness for her folks and the ranch she'd been raised on. But as they continued over the years, I eventually concluded the calls were what kept my wife in a constant state of low-grade depression. I'd prayed she would find joy in something, but little seemed to work. Her mother was always there to bring her back to a state of feeling inadequate and dissatisfied with her life.

It was while she was with her parents on their ranch that I woke up about 1:00 a.m. feeling so distraught I started praying for God's help. Specifically, I asked him why my wife couldn't trust me enough to let me know why she had driven our family so close to the edge of bankruptcy.

That's when I heard a voice.

Or should I say, *the* Voice.

As audible as any voice I've ever heard, it said only one thing: "You are blaming her for the very thing of which you are guilty with respect to me."

The translation of this statement in my mind: how could I blame her for not trusting me when I was guilty of not trusting the Lord?

A good question, actually, and not one I would have come up with on my own. Better yet, for me it was a game changer.

I stood alone that night knowing I had been both

accused and convicted of my brokenness and given the choice to be absolved of my shortcomings by a God who clearly wanted to be by my side to help me through the hardship in which I found myself. And so I answered the Voice. I told him I was sorry. I asked him for forgiveness. I asked for his help.

In short, I prayed and meant it!

I loved my sons. I very much thought I loved my wife. After twelve years now of marriage, I also clung to the hope she loved me at least enough to want to save our marriage. So in my mind there was but one available path by which this impasse could be put behind us: do whatever I could to hold the family together, then trust the Lord to do all that I was not capable of.

To that end, I repaid the debts, hired an attorney friend to negotiate a plea to resolve my wife's misdemeanors, then started marriage counseling with my wife to heal our family. This eventually took us back to the same part of the country from which my grandparents had purposely moved away almost seventy years earlier so that my wife could be closer to her parents.

If this did not in the end result in restoring our marriage, the move marked a new phase of my life journey during which God would guide me toward an even clearer understanding of his purposes than he had already. And to a joy, peace and love I'd given up hoping for. That is a tale for another time—or maybe another book.

But on this particular scorching afternoon several weeks later, the pain of it all was still fresh, and that's what I found myself thinking about as I leaned against the wall, waiting for my case to be called by Hewitt. That is, until the solitude of my mental rumination was interrupted.

"Jiminy Crickets!" I heard a nasally countrified voice announce to nobody in particular. "Well, all I can say is, it's hotter out here than a rooster dancing in the barnyard at noon and drier than a pig's fart."

With the turn of my head, I spotted the source of this sage if humorous rendering of the obvious. He was the sort of short, stooped-over old-timer I might have expected to find on the other end of such a comment. Unshaven. Wrinkled from too much time in the sun. Clothes that needed cleaning. A yellow smile missing a tooth or two.

I offered a somewhat whiter smile of my own and attempted to respond in kind. "Yep, hot enough to make even a horny toad go limp."

His eyebrows immediately lifted toward the wrinkles traversing his forehead, his wry smirk plainly trying to tell me, *Nice try, young feller!*

As if to drive home that I wasn't remotely in his class when it came to *country-speak*, he pointed to a man in his sixties standing some twenty feet away and chuckled. "Look at that fat old fart standing out there in the sun. Not to speak poorly of the dim-witted, but he must have a brain smaller than a bumblebee's balls not to have the sense God gave a toad to seek some shade. He's sweating more than a pig trying to pass a peach pit!"

I could only smile and nod to silently acknowledge I was clearly out of my league. But as I conceded defeat, I suddenly noticed that his assessment of the man he'd been pointing to was correct. Beyond sweating, the guy was also now swaying. Then he just collapsed where he stood, making no attempt to break his fall to the ground.

Odder still was that my new-found friend and I appeared to be the only ones who seemed to notice this guy, much less care. Which reminded me that I was at the vortex of that segment of humanity that gathers at all courthouses: the "don't bother me, I've got enough problems of my own" demographic.

By default, I guessed it would be up to my new friend and me to see what was going on with this man now sprawled on the ground like a clump of wet mud left to dry if not fry. But that assumption proved premature.

"Well, looks like it's time for me to shake a tail feather," my new friend informed me. "Hope he's okay."

Then he too disappeared, leaving just me to deal with the guy on the ground. As I approached, I saw that the man was clearly unconscious or maybe even dead. In fact, the only thing about him that I could see moving was the opaque-green foam oozing out the side of his mouth and down his unshaven cheek to drip on the hot concrete beneath his head.

The first thing I did was to crouch down to feel for a pulse, then bend down further to see if I could hear any breathing. I found evidence of neither, which caused my own heart to race and my mind to race even faster. As I was checking, I sensed someone's presence and looked up to see one of the court clerks kneeling beside me.

"Is he dead?" she asked.

"I don't know," I answered. "But he sure looks like he could be. He doesn't seem to be breathing."

We both called out for someone to call an ambulance. But I knew time was an important factor. If something was going to be done to help this man, we couldn't wait for medics to arrive. The clerk was looking at me with a face that screamed her own revulsion as she asked in a tone of voice that strongly suggested her answer, "Mouth-to-mouth?"

Looking at the man's foamy vomit, I knew my answer was the same as hers. I would have only added my vomit to the goop coming out of the guy's mouth, which wouldn't have helped either of us very much. Then I suddenly remembered some of the T.V. shows I'd watched over the years with cardiac arrest scenes where the actors always jolted the heart attack victim's chest with umpteen volts of electricity.

Lacking a power source, I knew the electric jolt wasn't going to happen. But perhaps a shock of some other kind could revive him. At that point I felt I had no choice. I rolled him on his back, clenched my fist, and hit the man on the chest right about where I thought his heart would be.

Wham!

The impact was almost hard enough to break his ribs, or so it felt like to me. But no response.

I tried it again.

Wham!

Again nothing.

Hmmm, maybe this guy really is dead, I told myself. *If that's the case, one or two more times won't hurt.*

I tried a third time, but this time did so while saying a prayer under my breath. *God, help me out here!*

Wham!

This time I got a different result. The man coughed.

Encouraged, I hit him one last time, but not as hard. The still unconscious man miraculously drew a breath—and coughed again. Then another breath and another. I fumbled again for a pulse and actually felt one.

As the guy continued to cough, some of the green foam in his mouth and throat spewed to splatter around on his face. Backing quickly away, I asked myself, *How could anyone ever want to be a doctor? Or for that matter, a mortician?*

Even so, I took this evidence of life in my patient to be an improvement and could only assume the clerk beside me did as well as we both retreated out of reach of his sputum spray. About then I saw a sheriff's deputy heading our direction in a run across the courtyard, obviously to see what was going on.

At this point, I knew I'd done all I could for this guy, so I said to the clerk in a low voice, "Okay, I'm out of here. Can you tell the deputy what's going on? I don't want to be around when this guy wakes up. You never know. I might have hurt him and don't need the lawsuit."

She nodded as I stood up and withdrew back into the crowd now forming. I didn't want the man to have any memory of me when he came to in case I'd bruised him or, even worse, cracked one of his ribs. The clerk seemed to understand and without a word let me know she had my back. As I walked away, I could hear her explaining to the approaching deputy what had happened.

By now the man on the ground had recovered consciousness enough to start talking. He appeared to be angry, though at nobody in particular other than perhaps the deputy bending over him in a crouched position. My former patient was saying things like, "What's going on? What are you doing? Who the %#&! knocked me out? Somebody's gonna get sued! You can count on that."

Hearing all that followed, I was glad I hadn't gone into medicine and even gladder to be several feet away hidden among other perspiring spectators who by then had gathered to gawk. The man was now trying to get up off the ground while the deputy was doing all he could to keep the man from exerting himself.

"You've probably had a heart attack," the deputy told the man calmly. "Please just lie still and stay calm. An ambulance is on the way."

It's interesting how life sometimes takes people in a direction you couldn't anticipate. My former patient was not having it. Ignoring the deputy, he continued trying to get up. Undoubtedly concerned about the man's well-being, the deputy leaned in further to prevent him from doing further injury to himself. That only made the man even angrier. Swinging at the officer, he clipped him on the chin.

"You *#@# cop!" he yelled. "Get your hands off me. I know my rights."

Funny how many times I've heard people say that last part about their rights. More often than not, just saying it was proof that in fact they didn't know their rights, much less the *limits* of those rights.

From that perspective, it was fascinating to watch how quickly things changed once the man informed the deputy of his "rights." After clipping the deputy on the chin, his foremost right promptly became his right to remain silent. A right of which he was failing miserably to take advantage.

Before the man knew what was happening, the deputy rolled him over and cuffed him. Even that didn't stop his tirade. He continued to swear at the deputy right up until the paramedics loaded him, cuffs and all, into the ambulance and carried him off to the hospital to be treated— and from there most likely to be booked for assault-and-battery on an officer.

While the whole thing hadn't worked out so well for my former patient, at least he'd left me mildly happy. For one thing, it was unlikely he could have swung at the officer like he did with any broken ribs. Better yet, if my prayer for him hadn't been answered, he might not have been able to swing at the officer at all.

Hmmm. That's pretty cool, I thought as I headed back to court, wondering if my case had been called yet.

I hoped not.

I most certainly did not want to have to do a day like this all over again tomorrow.

But even if it happened, I thought, should my response be anger?

After hearing the Voice in the kitchen a few nights before coupled with today's events, I'd have to say probably not.

The short course being that in all circumstances it

probably would always be best to just seek God's face and say, "Thank you!"

Do not be eager in your heart to be angry,
For anger resides in the bosom of fools.[3] *For those whom the Lord*
loves he disciplines, and he scourges every son whom he receives.[4]

Answer me when I call, O God of my righteousness! You have relieved me in my distress; be gracious to me and hear my prayer.[1]

∾

23

A DAY AT THE MATINÉE

Todd was a plumber. He had entered the profession a little over three years before and seemed to be doing well.

He also appeared to have reformed the bad habits of his youth. Since his last release from prison, he'd married a beautiful woman, had two precious little children, bought a charming small house, and minded his own business. Even to his parole officer, Todd appeared to be a success story on wheels seen only too rarely in his profession.

But that was not to last.

The sheriff's department, acting on a reliable informant's tip, about a plumber fitting Todd's description who was selling drugs out of his truck, got warrants to search Todd's service truck and his home.

In the home, they found nothing except Todd's wife, the babies taking their afternoon naps, and a small amount of cash under some socks in a dresser drawer. In the truck they found much more. The expected narcotics were tucked under the driver's seat—along with a videotape cartridge.

The deputies booked the drugs, cash, and videotape into evidence and arrested not only Todd but his wife. Based upon cash in the home and narcotics in the truck, the district attorney justified charging both spouses with a conspiracy to sell illicit drugs. So began their period of marital strife.

I met the couple because I'd been appointed by Judge Hewitt to represent Todd's wife. As the case unfolded, it became manifestly clear to me that until her home was raided by half-a-dozen officers with drawn guns, she had no idea her husband was involved in a second career—let alone that of a drug dealer.

She'd known Todd was a felon on parole when they met. But he'd convinced her that he'd turned away from his dark past. He went to work every day and seemed to make ample money as a plumber to support his family. They enjoyed barbecues with neighbors on weekends and on Sundays attended the church she and her parents had gone to since she was a little girl. With that life, she was more than content.

That she loved her husband became quickly evident to me, her concern always more for him than for herself. She was indeed an example of a woman standing by her man.

So when she was told that Todd not only had narcotics in his service vehicle but was charged with being a felon in possession of a firearm, she just knew that couldn't be true. At no time since she'd known him had there been a gun, much less narcotics, in their home. At least that she knew of. The drugs the sheriff's deputies had found must be someone else's. She wanted the court to know what a good man he'd become.

At one point, she even pleaded, "Please let the court know Todd was baptized a couple of years back. He was saved. He *is* saved. I know he is. I've lived with him. I know him."

In her heart, she had faith that by clearing Todd's good name, she also would be vindicated and cleared of all charges brought against her as a result of her connection with him. But she would soon learn just how wrong a person can be about another person they think they know very well.

From time to time in any courthouse, something will be scheduled in a particular court that everyone in the building is eager to observe. Typically, such events involve the appearance of a celebrity or sentencing of some notorious criminal. But on the afternoon when the preliminary hearing for Todd and his wife was scheduled, the courtroom was filled to capacity for quite a different reason.

The district attorney had let it be known he intended to establish probable cause that Todd was a felon on parole illegally in possession of a firearm by playing the video found under the seat of Todd's truck. The recording apparently showed Todd in possession of a gun. And the date stamp on the video placed the time frame within the period of his parole as well as his marriage.

But those legal technicalities were not what attracted such a crowd in the court that afternoon. It was the fact that this video starred none other than Todd himself engaged in a variety of sexual activities with a prostitute that included his use of a .44 Magnum handgun as a sex toy. The video had been shot on location in a cheap motel room, and the district attorney handling the case had let slip the rumor that the action scenes were better than anything that could be rented from the local adult book store.

By the time Todd and his wife were brought in from lockup, clerks, bailiffs, court reporters, and attorneys from around the courthouse had taken every available seat and were standing shoulder-to-shoulder along the walls and down some of the aisles to get a peek at the action. From the get-go, the district attorney's continuous smile and swagger made it clear he found it perversely exciting to be the designated producer for the afternoon's entertainment.

Judge Hewitt appeared equally pleased to be serving as master of ceremonies for the video premier as indicated by a smile he rarely displayed other than for the delivery of a drink to his table at the Elks Lodge. By the time Hewitt emerged from his chambers to take the bench, the room was almost festive. The only thing lacking was the popcorn.

Not sharing in the glee were Todd, Todd's wife, and me, seated between the couple. Todd's attorney, seated on Todd's far side, seemed more interested in the sudden notoriety the case had brought him than anything else. Though I'd given her a heads-up as to the video's alleged content, Todd's wife had not yet seen her husband's darker side and appeared confused and shocked by the interest of the crowd and overwhelmed by its size.

To kick off the hearing, pertinent objections and

motions were presented by both the husband's attorney and me—including our request that all unnecessary onlookers be ordered to vacate the courtroom. Judge Hewitt hastily denied them all and ordered that the video show commence.

From the dialogue, the movie's one and only scene appeared to tell the story of two men celebrating a successful drug transaction with a lady of the evening. The star of the film was Todd in the nude with an equally nude girl on the bed being filmed by an unidentified cameraman. All three members of the cast were laughing as Todd *au naturel* was seen pursuing the girl around the bed.

As the sex began in earnest, Todd and the prostitute continued to laugh and giggle on screen while at my side the breathing of Todd's wife became increasingly audible —at least to me. Tears spilled down her cheeks to form blotches of wetness on her jailhouse blouse as she started to sob almost silently but with a heaving chest that was desperately gulping for breath. Slowly, she bowed her head. Fortunately for her, she missed entirely the part in the film where the unknown cameraman laughingly handed her husband a handgun.

Meanwhile, the courtroom audience continued watching the film and cracking off-colored jokes, completely missing the reality that a woman's entire world was being absolutely shattered right under their noses. That was her husband on the screen. The father of their children. The man she went to church with. The man she loved and who she'd thought loved her.

But not anymore. She could no longer deny the truth

that she'd been used. That her whole life with Todd had been a lie. Had he ever even cared about her or their children?

At that moment with her face frozen in shock and tears mixed with mucous from her nose dripping to the floor, she appeared to be fast coming to a point where something had to be done or she was going to break right here in the courtroom.

Standing, I interrupted, "Objection, Your Honor. There's no need to continue this video. Again, we'll stipulate for purposes of this preliminary hearing that the video shows this co-defendant in possession of a handgun."

As expected, Todd's attorney quickly added, "We'll join in that, Your Honor."

But Judge Hewitt wasn't having it. That he was thoroughly enjoying the show was made clear by his annoyance at my rudeness in interrupting the good times with an inopportune objection. He struck his gavel loudly on his desk. "Overruled. I'm not going to have you guys complain later on appeal that we didn't see it all. Let it roll."

And so the video resumed. Which left me with what to do about Todd's wife. Something had to be done. The look on her face told me she was reaching a very bad, dark place. As her chest continued to heave, her eyes were beginning to stare blankly off into nowhere. In that moment, she seemed more like she wanted to die rather than live.

That's when it came to mind what Papa had said nearly thirty years before on his porch. "Son, no matter where your life takes you, always remember, if you have eyes willing to see and ears willing to hear, you will come to find you are never traveling alone."

Never traveling alone.

For reasons only God knows, it was then at the age of forty-five that I finally understood what Papa meant in a way that became personal. I also knew just what to do next.

As I put my arm around my client's shoulders, I leaned in to suggest in a whisper what had come to mind. I wanted us to talk to the Voice that had spoken to me in my kitchen late one night not so very long before. Without reservation, I knew the Spirit of Jesus was here with us in this very courtroom. All I had to do was ask and he would know what was best for my client.

"Look, you don't need to keep watching this or even listening to it," I whispered to my client. "If you like, I think it would be a good thing to pray. What say we talk to God for a while until this thing is done? He's here with us, you know."

Gratitude appeared on her face, but all her choking voice could muster through her tearful sobs was, "Yes, that would be good."

Tears came to my eyes at the thought that God too might be saying of my seeking him in the midst of this trial, "Yes, that would be good."

Strangely, I've wondered ever since if in my client's tears I was not also seeing my Lord crying tears of gladness that I had finally arrived at the place he and Papa both had undoubtedly hoped I'd reach much earlier in life. That place of awareness that, no matter where I was or was going to go, God would always be with me—and always had been.

Without more needing to be said, my client and I turned our chairs away from the screen and toward each other, bent our heads, and started a prayer that continued as the film and now-hideous laughter of that vile three-some continued to blare out for the pleasure of the room.

First, I thanked God for reminding us of his Spirit's presence even as we sat in Hewitt's court.

We asked for strength.

We asked for forgiveness of all who were involved in my client's pain.

We asked to be covered by God's grace.

We asked for God's protection from the enemy that like a roaring lion was seeking to destroy my client's marriage, family, and possibly even her life.

Eventually, we came around to asking that God's Spirit would vanquish all the evil that had taken up residence in Hewitt's courtroom that afternoon.

Suddenly, the district attorney's voice speaking above the video's soundtrack interrupted our prayer. Evidently even he'd had his fill and wanted to stop the film. With that, Hewitt reluctantly agreed, and the film mercifully stopped.

At that point, it was as though Todd's wife and I were awakened from a trance that had only lasted about fifteen minutes but seemed like so much longer.

As we opened our eyes, I will never forget my sense of amazement. All the voyeurs who had been in the room were gone! The only people left were those people essential to the proceedings at hand.

When had all the others left? More importantly, *why* had they left?

Some might respond, *Who knows and who cares?*

To which I would respond, *He does!*

I have no doubt in my mind that Jesus, who promised that those who mourn will be lifted to safety,[2] had answered our prayers.

A miracle?

Maybe what we call a miracle is really only the label we give to those events in our life where we are privileged and amazed to witness God actually doing what he promised us he will do for us. In how many ways has he tried to get us to believe that he really is "our refuge and strength, a very present help in trouble?"[3]

The truth is that people like me more often than not lack the faith to really believe it. So when God does come through in our lives, we call it coincidence or luck or anything other than what it really is—a promise fulfilled yet again by a God who is good and who really does love us.

And with my client, he wasn't done yet. After the video stopped, the district attorney made a motion to dismiss all charges against my client. Hewitt granted the motion, something he almost never did. She left the room that day with a calm about her I would never have imagined possible at such a horrible moment in her life. While I never saw her again, witnessing such a peace come over her that was beyond my understanding is a memory that has never left me.

Oh, the beauty God can cause to rise from the ashes of tragedy in response to our prayers!

That is my Papa's God. The same God who on that day in court finally brought me around to realizing that he is also *my* God. A patient God who is with me today. A God who has been with me wherever I've ever been in my life.

Most interesting to me was that this was a realization thirty years in the making. All started by a thought Papa had let drop like a pebble to roll around in my head when he left me behind on the porch that night, knowing I was only starting my journey as his was drawing to a close.

"Son, no matter where your life takes you, always remember, if you have eyes willing to see and ears willing to hear, you will come to find *you are never traveling alone.*"

The Lord is near. Be anxious for nothing, but in everything by prayer … let your requests be made known to God. and the peace of God, which surpasses all comprehension, will guard your hearts and your minds in Christ Jesus.[4]

For from days of old they have not heard ... by ear, or has the eye seen a God besides you, who acts on behalf of the one who waits for him. [1]
For the Lord knows the way of the righteous, but the way of the wicked will perish. [2]

~

24

THE CLOSING ARGUMENT

We have now arrived at the end of these Tales. Thank you for joining me on this leg of the journey.

As we now prepare to go our separate ways—at least for the time being—let me leave you with my hope that, if you haven't already, you too will discover what I didn't for so long. In the pebble that Papa left me with that night to ponder, the operative word I'd missed for so long was "willing." It took me nearly thirty years to become *willing* to hear and *willing* to see that no matter where I found myself in life, God was always there with me.

It is this willingness that is our choice alone to make. In fact, it really is the *only* choice we've all been placed on this earth to make that truly matters. In the case of many, it is a willingness to ask God to show you he is very real, very present and very much loves you. It is also a willingness to receive his answer. So ... ask him. In the privacy of your home without anyone around, simply ask. He knows you better than you know yourself. Leave it to him to show you his love for you in a way that will speak to you. The only thing he requires of you before this will happen is that you, in your heart, be honestly *willing* to know the truth about his presence in this world. And, be *willing* to let him into your world.

To refuse to take this small—yet, incredibly important —step makes no sense. Our lives here on earth are finite, while the eternal that is certain to follow for each of us is infinite.

Imagine being cloistered in a cabin that is your world. The windows you keep shuttered and there is only one door that you also keep closed knowing with dread that one day you will have to walk through it when you pass away. Then further imagine receiving word that a God who loves you is on the porch and only wants to be let in to share your world—i.e., cabin—with you. You are told he wants you to allow him in to help you, to open the windows of your world and let you see what is beyond the confines of your immediate surroundings into that which is eternal. A very personal God who wants nothing more than to make your world a better and brighter place, both now and after you cross the cabin's threshold into the eternal beyond. All you have to do is to be willing to open the door and invite him in to share your world while he remains available to you. Again, the choice is yours.

Why wouldn't you at least want to make the effort to call out to the one who you have been told is on your porch to at least find out if, indeed, he really is there? Otherwise, you may come to learn that he loved you so much as to respect your choice to remain ignorant of his presence. Thus, when the time arrives for you to have to cross that threshold, you risk learning quickly that in deference to your decision he has departed and left you with your choice to confront the eternal alone. To avoid such a fate, logic and reason suggest that you would—and that you should—at the very least make the effort to seek his face while he remains on your cabin porch and attempt to draw near to him by inviting him in while time remains.

Which brings me to my final suggestion: try to not take as long as I did to make that choice. After all, life can go by pretty quickly, and we never really know for certain how long we will have to make the choice to acknowledge Jesus Christ as our Lord. All we know for certain is that some day each of us will be required to leave our cabin.

Take Judge Hewitt for instance. Shortly after he had amused himself and others at my client's expense, he was found dead in his fishing boat while on vacation somewhere down in Mexico. Word had it he'd gotten so drunk, he tripped and hit his head on one of the rope cleats at the rear of his boat. As was the case with his Elks Lodge drinking buddy, P. Cummings, it seems Hewitt never knew what hit him.

I was told only a few came around to his memorial to mourn his passing—perhaps even fewer than had gathered in his court that day to enjoy the matinée.

From an eternal perspective, I can only hope that for him it had all been worth the cost of admission.

Somehow, I doubt it.

The conclusion, when all has been heard, is: fear God and keep His commandments, because this applies to every person. For God will bring every act to judgment, everything which is hidden, whether it is good or evil.[3]

Papa

Your word is a lamp to my feet and a light to my path. [1]

∼

ABOUT THE AUTHOR

Cliff Nichols has practiced law for nearly thirty-five years. A former research associate at The Heritage Foundation, he graduated from UCLA summa cum laude, Phi Beta Kappa with a bachelor's degree in economics. He received his juris doctorate degree cum laude at Northwestern Pritzker University School of Law, where he served as a member of the board of editors of the *Northwestern University Law Review*.

Mr. Nichols is also a seasoned political commentator whose editorials have been published locally by the Santa Monica Daily Press, nationally by Townhall.com, and have been cited in both the *Drudge Report* and Hillsdale College's monthly publication *Imprimis*. A collection of his more recent editorials may be found at www.cliffordnichols.com. Any comments, suggestions, or questions regarding this book or any of his editorials may be directed to him at cliff@cliffordnichols.com. He also may be followed on Twitter @Cliff1Nichols and on Facebook.

At the end of the day—notwithstanding all the places, experiences and people he has encountered—he still regards his grandfather's parting words as some of the best advice he's ever received:

"Son, no matter where your life takes you, always remember, if you have eyes willing to see and ears willing to hear, you will come to find you are never traveling alone."

~

The grace of the Lord Jesus be with all. Amen.[2]

Without consultation, plans are frustrated, but with many counselors they succeed.[1]

ACKNOWLEDGMENTS

First and foremost, I thank God for moving me to write these Tales.

Then second only to God, I thank my wife Lynda for reading, correcting, and proofing them more times than any human should have to endure.

Next, my sincerest gratitude goes out to my editor, Jeanette Windle, without whose expertise and professionalism—not to mention insightful opinions—this work would never have been made possible.

Last but by no means least, I want to express my sincere appreciation to all my friends and experts—each of you knows who you are—for so generously spending your time, talents, and encouragement to make this book far better than it would have been in your absence, including, among others, Robert N., Willie H., Kim G., Bob H., Leon L., Michael M., Amanda P., Alley B., Justin A., and Skip T.

Listen to counsel and accept discipline, that you may be wise the rest of your days.[2]

A Few Last Thoughts Before We Say Goodbye

A Request to You from the Author

Dear Reader,

I would like to thank you for reading these Tales. My sincere hope is that you enjoyed reading them as much as I did writing them.

If so, would you please consider posting a review of A Barrister's Tales on Amazon?

I would be honored, and on a personal level, I will very much appreciate receiving your feedback.

Thank you,

Cliff Nichols

Link To Write Your Review

And ...

Send this book
as a gift to a friend
who is seeking God...
or perhaps should be?

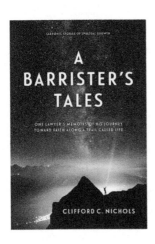

If you do send this book to a loved one, you never know. The consequences could be eternal...

Just snap the QR code to Amazon below!

And ...

CONSIDER ANOTHER BOOK
BY CLIFF NICHOLS

If you...

a) enjoy satire;

b) appreciate humor;

c) enjoy taking a poke
   at progressives; and

d) consider yourself to be an
   all-around cool human,

then... **you might not
loathe this book!**

So... scan this QR code and do the right thing.

But if that's not you, do your best
to not have a miserable day.

Or ...

FOR A LIMITED TIME!

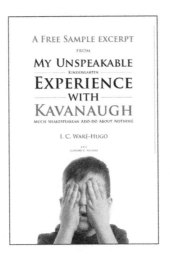

You can get a **FREE excerpt** of
*My Unspeakable Kindergarten Experience
with Kavanaugh* when you sign up
to receive Cliff's latest updates!

Simply scan the QR code:

Goodbye Now

&

May your journey from here be blessed.

NOTES

Dedication

1. Isaiah 32:8
2. Proverbs 16:9

Opening Argument

1. Micah 6:8

A Note from the Author

1. Proverbs 19:21
2. John 8:32

The Truth Will Set You Free

1. Psalm 139:1-4
2. 2 Corinthians 4:17-18
3. John 8:31-32

1. A Seed Planted

1. Matthew 13:31-32
2. Matthew 13:22

2. The Genesis of It All

1. Genesis 1:26
2. Proverbs 22:6

3. An Uphill Climb

1. Habakkuk 3:19
2. Psalm 40:2

4. Desperados, Why Don't You Come to Your Senses?

1. Psalm 40:14
2. Psalm 19:1

5. Run Jane Run, See Jane Run

1. Proverbs 7:7
2. Psalm 120:2

6. A Spectator's Peril

1. Psalm 31:2
2. Psalm 107:29

7. An Invitation I Couldn't Refuse

1. Psalm 12:2
2. Job 15:31

8. Sometimes Guacamole Can Roll Uphill

1. Proverbs 29:23
2. Obadiah 1:3-4

9. Cutting Corners

1. Deuteronomy 10:21
2. Psalm 91:10-11

10. My New Family

1. Romans 5:3-5
2. James 1:2-4

11. An Offer of Help Postponed

1. Jeremiah 17:5
2. Proverbs 4:5

12. Help from a Crippled Angel

1. 2 Kings 6:17
2. Ephesians 6:10-12
3. Matthew 4:11

13. Hooking Up with Mr. Murder

1. Ecclesiastes 10:3
2. Ecclesiastes 10:1

14. Better Late than Never, But Better Never Late

1. Isaiah 24:9
2. Jeremiah 40:4

15. Perhaps Shakespeare Said It Best

1. Proverbs 30-32
2. Ecclesiastes 2:19

16. The One Night Stand

1. Proverbs 5:8-9
2. Proverbs 5:3-5

17. What Evil Is

1. 1 Peter 5:8
2. James 4:7
3. Proverbs 1:33

18. Should a Murder Matter?

1. Proverbs 4:19
2. Job 18:5,7

19. Sometimes the Good Go Bad

1. Psalm 9:16
2. Psalm 7:15-16

20. How Injustice is Served

1. Deuteronomy 16:19-20
2. Isaiah 59:14
3. Psalm 64:6

21. A Record Broken

1. Ecclesiastes 8:9-10
2. Matthew 18:15-17
3. Ephesians 6:12-13
4. Hebrews 5: 11-14
5. Hebrews 11:6
6. Psalm 37:28
7. Galatians 6:7

22. Hard Knocks Are Sometimes Good

1. James 1:19
2. Job 5:2
3. Ecclesiastes 7:9
4. Hebrew 12:6

23. A Day at the Matinée

1. Psalm 4:1
2. Job 5:11
3. Psalm 46:1
4. Philippians 4:4-7

24. The Closing Argument

1. Isaiah 64:4
2. Psalm 1:6
3. Ecclesiastes 12:13-14

About the Author

1. Psalm 119:105
2. Revelation 22:21

Acknowledgments

1. Proverbs 15:22
2. Proverbs 19:20

Made in the USA
Middletown, DE
25 July 2023

35700763R00186